I0162165

Red Cotton Night-Cap Country by Robert Browning

or TURF AND TOWERS

Robert Browning is one of the most significant Victorian Poets and, of course, English Poetry.

Much of his reputation is based upon his mastery of the dramatic monologue although his talents encompassed verse plays and even a well-regarded essay on Shelley during a long and prolific career.

He was born on May 7th, 1812 in Walmouth, London. Much of his education was home based and Browning was an eclectic and studious student, learning several languages and much else across a myriad of subjects, interests and passions.

Browning's early career began promisingly. The fragment from his intended long poem Pauline brought him to the attention of Dante Gabriel Rossetti, and was followed by Paracelsus, which was praised by both William Wordsworth and Charles Dickens. In 1840 the difficult Sordello, which was seen as willfully obscure, brought his career almost to a standstill.

Despite these artistic and professional difficulties his personal life was about to become immensely fulfilling. He began a relationship with, and then married, the older and better known Elizabeth Barrett. This new foundation served to energise his writings, his life and his career.

During their time in Italy they both wrote much of their best work. With her untimely death in 1861 he returned to London and thereafter began several further major projects.

The collection Dramatis Personae (1864) and the book-length epic poem The Ring and the Book (1868-69) were published and well received; his reputation as a venerated English poet now assured.

Robert Browning died in Venice on December 12th, 1889.

Index of Contents

TO MISS THACKERAY

This poem, dated January 23rd, 1873, was published in the early summer of the same year. Browning had been staying with his sister at St. Aubin, in Normandy, and there met Miss Thackeray, who was to tell a tale of the White Cotton Night-cap Country, but a tragedy then just coming to a culmination in the courts supplied Browning with the more suggestive title which he adopted. Mr. Cooke records:—

"In the poem as written the names of the actors and places were correctly given, but when the poem was being revised in proof-sheets they were changed from prudential reasons, because the last act in the tragedy occurred only a brief period prior to the writing of the poem.

"Browning submitted the proof-sheets of the poem to his friend Lord Coleridge, then the English Attorney-General, afterwards Chief Justice, who thought that a case of libel might lie for what was said, however improbable such action might be. He accordingly changed the names to fictitious ones. It was the year following this, and the publication of the poem, that the appeal against the judgment in favor of the will of Mellerio was dismissed, and the case finally set at rest in harmony with the conclusion reached by the poet."

In the second edition of her Hand-Book Mrs. Orr gives the correct names, as furnished to her by Browning himself. These names will be found in the notes at the end of this volume.

RED COTTON NIGHT-CAP COUNTRY

I

And so, here happily we meet, fair friend!
Again once more, as if the years rolled back
And this our meeting-place were just that Rome
Out in the champaign, say, o'er-rioted
By verdure, ravage, and gay winds that war
Against strong sunshine settled to his sleep;
Or on the Paris Boulevard, might it prove,
You and I came together saunteringly,
Bound for some shop-front in the Place Vendôme—
Goldsmithy and Golconda mine, that makes
"The Firm—Miranda" blazed about the world—
Or, what if it were London, where my toe
Trespassed upon your flounce? "Small blame," you smile,
Seeing the Staircase Party in the Square
Was Small and Early, and you broke no rib.
Even as we met where we have met so oft,
Now meet we on this unpretending beach
Below the little village: little, ay!
But pleasant, may my gratitude subjoin?
Meek, hitherto un-Murrayed bathing-place,
Best loved of seacoast-nookful Normandy!
That, just behind you, is mine own hired house:
With right of pathway through the field in front,
No prejudice to all its growth unsheaved
Of emerald luzern bursting into blue.
Be sure I keep the path that hugs the wall,
Of mornings, as I pad from door to gate!
Yon yellow—what if not wild—mustard flower?—

Of that, my naked sole makes lawful prize,
Bruising the acrid aromatics out,
Till, what they preface, good salt savors sting
From, first, the sifted sands, then sands in slab,
Smooth save for pipy wreath-work of the worm:
(Granite and mussel-shell are ground alike
To glittering paste,—the live worm troubles yet.)
Then, dry and moist, the varech limit-line,
Burnt cinder-black, with brown uncrumpled swathe
Of berried softness, sea-swoln thrice its size;
And, lo, the wave protrudes a lip at last,
And flecks my foot with froth, nor tempts in vain.

Such is Saint-Rambert, wilder very much
Than Joyeux, that famed Joyous-Gard of yours,
Some five miles farther down; much homelier too—
Right for me,—right for you the fine and fair!
Only, I could endure a transfer—wrought
By angels famed still, through our countryside,
For weights they fetched and carried in old time
When nothing like the need was—transfer, just
Of Joyeux church, exchanged for yonder prig,
Our brand-new stone cream-colored masterpiece.

Well—and you know, and not since this one year,
The quiet seaside country? So do I:
Who like it, in a manner, just because
Nothing is prominently likable
To vulgar eye without a soul behind,
Which, breaking surface, brings before the ball
Of sight, a beauty buried everywhere.
If we have souls, know how to see and use,
One place performs, like any other place,
The proper service every place on earth
Was framed to furnish man with: serves alike
To give him note that, through the place he sees,
A place is signified he never saw,
But, if he lack not soul, may learn to know.
Earth's ugliest walled and ceiled imprisonment
May suffer, through its single rent in roof,
Admittance of a cataract of light
Beyond attainment through earth's palace-panes
Pinholed athwart their windowed filigree
By twinklings sobered from the sun outside.
Doubtless the High Street of our village here
Imposes hardly as Rome's Corso could:
And our projected race for sailing-boats
Next Sunday, when we celebrate our Saint,

Falls very short of that attractiveness,
That artistry in festive spectacle,
Paris ensures you when she welcomes back
(When shall it be?) the Assembly from Versailles;
While the best fashion and intelligence
Collected at the counter of our Mayor
(Dry-goods he deals in, grocery beside)
What time the post-bag brings the news from Vire,—
I fear me much, it scarce would hold its own,
That circle, that assorted sense and wit,
With Five-o'clock Tea in a house we know.

Still, 'tis the check that gives the leap its lift.
The nullity of cultivated souls,
Even advantaged by their news from Vire,
Only conduces to enforce the truth
That, thirty paces off, this natural blue
Broods o'er a bag of secrets, all unbroached,
Beneath the bosom of the placid deep,
Since first the Post Director sealed them safe;
And formidable I perceive this fact—
Little Saint-Rambert touches the great sea.
From London, Paris, Rome, where men are men,
Not mice, and mice not Mayors presumably,
Thought scarce may leap so fast, alight so far.
But this is a pretence, you understand,
Disparagement in play, to parry thrust
Of possible objector: nullity
And ugliness, the taunt be his, not mine
Nor yours,—I think we know the world too well!
Did you walk hither, jog it by the plain,
Or jaunt it by the highway, braving bruise
From springless and uncushioned vehicle?
Much, was there not, in place and people both,
To lend an eye to? and what eye like yours—
The learned eye is still the loving one!
Our land; its quietude, productiveness,
Is length and breadth of grain-crop, meadow-ground,
Its orchards in the pasture, farms a-field,
And hamlets on the road-edge, naught you missed
Of one and all the sweet rusticities!
From stalwart strider by the wagon-side,
Brightening the acre with his purple blouse,
To those dark-featured comely women-folk,
Healthy and tall, at work, and work indeed,
On every cottage doorstep, plying brisk
Bobbins that bob you ladies out such lace!
Oh, you observed! and how that nimble play

Of finger formed the sole exception, bobbed
The one disturbance to the peace of things,
Where nobody esteems it worth his while,
If time upon the clock-face goes asleep,
To give the rusted hands a helpful push.
Nobody lifts an energetic thumb
And index to remove some dead and gone
Notice which, posted on the barn, repeats
For truth what two years' passage made a lie.
Still is for sale, next June, that same château
With all its immobilities,—were sold
Duly next June behind the last but last;
And, woe's me, still placards the Emperor
His confidence in war he means to wage,
God aiding and the rural populace.
No: rain and wind must rub the rags away
And let the lazy land untroubled snore.

Ah, in good truth? and did the drowsihead
So suit, so soothe the learned loving eye,
That you were minded to confer a crown,
(Does not the poppy boast such?)—call the land
By one slow hither-thither stretching, fast
Subsiding-into-slumber sort of name,
Symbolic of the place and people too,
"White Cotton Night-cap Country?" Excellent!
For they do, all, dear women young and old,
Upon the heads of them bear notably
This badge of soul and body in repose;
Nor its fine thimble fits the acorn-top,
Keeps woolly ward above that oval brown,
Its placid feature, more than muffler makes
A safeguard, circumvents intelligence
In—what shall evermore be named and famed,
If happy nomenclature aught avail,
"White Cotton Night-cap Country."

Do I hear—
Oh, better, very best of all the news—
You mean to catch and cage the wingèd word,
And make it breed and multiply at home
Till Norman idlesse stock our England too?
Normandy shown minute yet magnified
In one of those small books, the truly great,
We never know enough, yet know so well?
How I foresee the cursive diamond-dints,—
Composite pen that plays the pencil too,—
As, touch the page and up the glamour goes,

And filmily o'er grain-crop, meadow-ground,
O'er orchard in the pasture, farm a-field,
And hamlet on the road-edge, floats and forms
And falls, at lazy last of all, the Cap
That crowns the country! we, awake outside,
Farther than ever from the imminence
Of what cool comfort, what close coverture
Your magic, deftly weaving, shall surround
The unconscious captive with. Be theirs to drowse
Trammelled, and ours to watch the trammel-trick!
Ours be it, as we con the book of books,
To wonder how is winking possible!

All hail, "White Cotton Night-cap Country," then!
And yet, as on the beach you promise book,—
On beach, mere razor-edge 'twixt earth and sea,
I stand at such a distance from the world
That 'tis the whole world which obtains regard,
Rather than any part, though part presumed
A perfect little province in itself,
When wayfare made acquaintance first therewith.
So standing, therefore, on this edge of things,
What if the backward glance I gave, return
Loaded with other spoils of vagrancy
Than I dispatched it for, till I propose
The question—puzzled by the sudden store
Officious fancy plumps beneath my nose—
"Which sort of Night-cap have you glorified?"

You would be gracious to my ignorance:
What other Night-cap than the normal one?—
Old honest guardian of man's head and hair
In its elastic yet continuous, soft,
No less persisting, circumambient gripe,—
Night's notice, life is respited from day!
Its form and fashion vary, suiting so
Each seasonable want of youth and age.
In infancy, the rosy naked ball
Of brain, and that faint golden fluff it bears,
Are smothered from disaster,—nurses know
By what foam-fabric; but when youth succeeds,
The sterling value of the article
Discards adornment, cap is cap henceforth
Unfeathered by the futile row on row.
Manhood strains hard a sturdy stocking-stuff
O'er well-deserving head and ears: the cone
Is tassel-tipt, commendably takes pride,
Announcing workday done and wages pouched,

And liberty obtained to sleep, nay, snore.
Unwise, he peradventure shall essay
The sweets of independency for once—
Waive its advantage on his wedding-night:
Fool, only to resume it, night the next,
And never part companionship again.
Since, with advancing years, night's solace soon
Intrudes upon the daybreak dubious life
Persuades it to appear the thing it is
Half-sleep; and so, encroaching more and more,
It lingers long past the abstemious meal
Of morning, and, as prompt to serve, precedes
The supper-summons, gruel grown a feast.
Finally, when the last sleep finds the eye
So tired it cannot even shut itself,
Does not a kind domestic hand unite
Friend to friend, lid from lid to part no more,
Consigned alike to that receptacle
So bleak without, so warm and white within?

"Night-caps, night's comfort of the human race:
Their usage may be growing obsolete,
Still, in the main, the institution stays.
And though yourself may possibly have lived,
And probably will die, undignified—
The Never-night-capped—more experienced folk
Laugh you back answer—What should Night-cap be
Save Night-cap pure and simple? Sorts of such?
Take cotton for the medium, cast an eye
This side to comfort, lambswool, or the like,
That side to frilly cambric costliness,
And all between proves Night-cap proper." Add
"Fiddle!" and I confess the argument.

Only, your ignoramus here again
Proceeds as tardily to recognize
Distinctions: ask him what a fiddle means,
And "Just a fiddle" seems the apt reply.
Yet, is not there, while we two pace the beach,
This blessed moment, at your Kensington,
A special Fiddle-Show and rare array
Of all the sorts were ever set to cheek,
'Stablished on clavicle, sawn bow-hand-wise,
Or touched lute-fashion and forefinger-plucked?
I doubt not there be duly catalogued
Achievements all and some of Italy,
Guarnerius, Straduarius,—old and new,
Augustly rude, refined to finicking,

This mammoth with his belly full of blare,
That mouse of music—inch-long silvery wheeze,
And here a specimen has effloresced
Into the scroll-head, there subsides supreme,
And with the tailpiece satisfies mankind.
Why should I speak of woods, grains, stains and streaks,
The topaz varnish or the ruby gum?
We preferably pause where tickets teach,
"Over this sample would Corelli croon,
Grieving, by minors, like the cushat-dove,
Most dulcet Giga, dreamiest Saraband."
"From this did Paganini comb the fierce
Electric sparks, or to tenuity
Pull forth the inmost wailing of the wire—
No cat-gut could swoon out so much of soul!"

Three hundred violin-varieties
Exposed to public view! And dare I doubt
Some future enterprise shall give the world
Quite as remarkable a Night-cap-show?
Methinks, we, arm-in-arm, that festal day,
Pace the long range of relics shrined aright,
Framed, glazed, each cushioned curiosity,
And so begin to smile and to inspect:
"Pope's sickly head-sustainment, damped with dews
Wrung from the all-unfair fight: such a frame—
Though doctor and the devil helped their best—
Fought such a world that, waiving doctor's help,
Had the mean devil at its service too!
Voltaire's imperial velvet! Hogarth eyed
The thumb-nail record of some alley-phiz,
Then chucklingly clapped yonder cosiness
On pate, and painted with true flesh and blood!
Poor hectic Cowper's soothing sarsnet-stripe!"
And so we profit by the catalogue,
Somehow our smile subsiding more and more,
Till we decline into ... but no! shut eyes
And hurry past the shame uncoffined here,
The hangman's toilet! If we needs must trench,
For science' sake which craves completeness still,
On the sad confine, not the district's self,
The object that shall close review may be ...
Well, it is French, and here are we in France:
It is historic, and we live to learn,
And try to learn by reading story-books.
It is an incident of 'Ninety-two,
And, twelve months since, the Commune had the sway.
Therefore resolve that, after all the Whites

Presented you, a solitary Red
Shall pain us both, a minute and no more!
Do not you see poor Louis pushed to front
Of palace-window, in persuasion's name,
A spectacle above the howling mob
Who tasted, as it were, with tiger-smack,
The outstart, the first spurt of blood on brow,
The Phrygian symbol, the new crown of thorns,
The Cap of Freedom? See the feeble mirth
At odds with that half-purpose to be strong
And merely patient under misery!
And note the ejaculation, ground so hard
Between his teeth, that only God could hear,
As the lean pale proud insignificance
With the sharp-featured liver-worried stare
Out of the two gray points that did him stead,
And passed their eagle-owner to the front
Better than his mob-elbowed undersize, —
The Corsican lieutenant commented,
"Had I but one good regiment of my own,
How soon should volleys to the due amount
Lay stiff upon the street-flags this canaille!
As for the droll there, he that plays the king,
And screws out smile with a Red night-cap on,
He 's done for! somebody must take his place."
White Cotton Night-cap Country: excellent!
Why not Red Cotton Night-cap Country too?

"Why not say swans are black and blackbirds white,
Because the instances exist?" you ask.
"Enough that white, not red, predominates.
Is normal, typical, in cleric phrase
Quod semel, semper, et ubique." Here,
Applying such a name to such a land,
Especially you find inopportune,
Impertinent, my scruple whether white
Or red describes the local color best.
"Let be," (you say,) "the universe at large
Supplied us with exceptions to the rule,
So manifold, they bore no passing-by, —
Little Saint-Rambert has conserved at least
The pure tradition: white from head to heel,
Where is a hint of the ungracious hue?
See, we have traversed with hop, step, and jump,
From heel to head, the main-street in a trice,
Measured the garment (help my metaphor!)
Not merely criticised the cap, forsooth;
And were you pricked by that collecting-itch,

That pruriency for writing o'er your reds,
'Rare, rarer, rarest, not rare but unique,'—
The shelf, Saint-Rambert, of your cabinet,
Unlabelled,—virginal, no Rahab-thread
For blushing-token of the spy's success,—
Would taunt with vacancy, I undertake!
What, yonder is your best apology,
Pretence at most approach to naughtiness,
Impingement of the ruddy on the blank?
This is the criminal Saint-Rambertese
Who smuggled in tobacco, half-a-pound!
The Octroi found it out and fined the wretch.
This other is the culprit who dispatched
A hare, he thought a hedgehog, (clods obstruct,)
Unfurnished with Permission for the Chase!
As to the womankind—renounce from those
The hope of getting a companion-tinge,
First faint touch promising romantic fault!"

Enough: there stands Red Cotton Night-cap shelf—
A cavern's ostentatious vacancy—
My contribution to the show; while yours—
Whites heap your row of pegs from every hedge
Outside, and house inside Saint-Rambert here—
We soon have come to end of. See, the church
With its white steeple gives your challenge point,
Perks as it were the night-cap of the town,
Starchedly warrants all beneath is matched
By all above, one snowy innocence!

You put me on my mettle. British maid
And British man, suppose we have it out
Here in the fields, decide the question so?
Then, British fashion, shake hands hard again,
Go home together, friends the more confirmed
That one of us—assuredly myself—
Looks puffy about eye, and pink at nose?
Which "pink" reminds me that the arduousness
We both acknowledge in the enterprise,
Claims, counts upon a large and liberal
Acceptance of as good as victory
In whatsoever just escapes defeat.
You must be generous, strain point, and call
Victory, any the least flush of pink
Made prize of, labelled scarlet for the nonce—
Faintest pretension to be wrong and red
And picturesque, that varies by a splotch
The righteous flat of insipidity.

Quick to the quest, then—forward, the firm foot!
Onward, the quarry-overtaking eye!
For, what is this, by way of march-tune, makes
The musicalest buzzing at my ear
By reassurance of that promise old,
Though sins as scarlet they shall be as wool?
Whence—what fantastic hope do I deduce?
I am no Liebig: when the dyer dyes
A texture, can the red dye prime the white?
And if we washed well, wrung the texture hard,
Would we arrive, here, there and everywhere,
At a fierce ground beneath the surface meek?

I take the first chance, rub to threads what rag
Shall flutter snowily in sight. For see!
Already these few yards upon the rise,
Our back to brave Saint-Rambert, how we reach
The open, at a dozen steps or strides!
Turn round and look about, a breathing-while!
There lie, outspread at equidistance, thorpes
And villages and towns along the coast,
Distinguishable, each and all alike,
By white persistent Night-cap, spire on spire.
Take the left: yonder town is—what say you
If I say "Londres"? Ay, the mother-mouse
(Reversing fable, as truth can and will)
Which gave our mountain of a London birth!
This is the Conqueror's country, bear in mind,
And Londres-district blooms with London-pride.
Turn round; La Roche, to right, where oysters thrive:
Monlieu—the lighthouse is a telegraph;
This, full in front, Saint-Rambert; then succeeds
Villeneuve, and Pons the Young with Pons the Old,
And—ere faith points to Joyeux, out of sight,
A little nearer—oh, La Ravissante!

There now is something like a Night-cap spire,
Donned by no ordinary Notre-Dame!
For, one of the three safety-guards of France,
You front now, lady! Nothing intercepts
The privilege, by crow-flight, two miles far.
She and her sisters Lourdes and La Salette
Are at this moment hailed the cynosure
Of poor dear France, such waves have buffeted
Since she eschewed infallibility
And chose to steer by the vague compass-box.
This same midsummer month, a week ago,

Was not the memorable day observed
For reinstatement of the misused Three
In old supremacy forevermore?
Did not the faithful flock in pilgrimage
By railway, diligence, and steamer—nay,
On foot with staff and scrip, to see the sights
Assured them? And I say best sight was here:
And nothing justified the rival Two
In their pretension to equality;
Our folk laid out their ticket-money best,
And wiseliest, if they walked, wore shoe away;
Not who went farther only to fare worse.
For, what was seen at Lourdes and La Salette
Except a couple of the common cures
Such as all three can boast of, any day?
While here it was, here and by no means there,
That the Pope's self sent two great real gold crowns
As thick with jewelry as thick could stick,
His present to the Virgin and her Babe—
Provided for—who knows not?—by that fund,
Count Alessandro Sforza's legacy,
Which goes to crown some Virgin every year.
But this year, poor Pope was in prison-house,
And money had to go for something else;
And therefore, though their present seemed the Pope's,
The faithful of our province raised the sum
Preached and prayed out of—nowise purse alone.
Gentle and simple paid in kind, not cash,
The most part: the great lady gave her brooch,
The peasant-girl, her hairpin; 't was the rough
Bluff farmer mainly who,—admonished well
By wife to care lest his new colewort-crop
Stray sorrowfully sparse like last year's seed,—
Lugged from reluctant pouch the fifty-franc,
And had the Curés hope that rain would cease.
And so, the sum in evidence at length,
Next step was to obtain the donative
By the spontaneous bounty of the Pope—
No easy matter, since his Holiness
Had turned a deaf ear, long and long ago,
To much entreaty on our Bishop's part,
Commendably we boast. "But no," quoth he,
"Image and image needs must take their turn:
Here stand a dozen as importunate."
Well, we were patient; but the cup ran o'er
When—who was it pressed in and took the prize
But our own offset, set far off indeed
To grow by help of our especial name,

She of the Ravissante—in Martinique!
"What!" cried our patience at the boiling-point,
"The daughter crowned, the mother's head goes bare?
Bishop of Raimbaux!"—that 's our diocese—
"Thou hast a summons to repair to Rome,
Be efficacious at the Council there:
Now is the time or never! Right our wrong!
Hie thee away, thou valued Morillon,
And have the promise, thou who hast the vote!"
So said, so done, so followed in due course
(To cut the story short) this festival,
This famous Twenty-second, seven days since.

Oh, but you heard at Joyeux! Pilgrimage,
Concourse, procession with, to head the host,
Cardinal Mirecourt, quenching lesser lights:
The leafy street-length through, decked end to end
With August-strippage, and adorned with flags,
That would have waved right well but that it rained
Just this picked day, by some perversity.
And so were placed, on Mother and on Babe,
The pair of crowns: the Mother's, you must see!
Miranda, the great Paris goldsmith, made
The marvel,—he 's a neighbor: that 's his park
Before you, tree-topped wall we walk toward.
His shop it was turned out the masterpiece,
Probably at his own expenditure;
Anyhow, his was the munificence
Contributed the central and supreme
Splendor that crowns the crown itself, The Stone.
Not even Paris, ransacked, could supply
That gem: he had to forage in New York,
This jeweller, and country-gentleman,
And most undoubted devotee beside!
Worthily wived, too: since his wife it was
Bestowed "with friendly hand"—befitting phrase!
The lace which trims the coronation-robe—
Stiff wear—a mint of wealth on the brocade.
Do go and see what I saw yesterday!
And, for that matter, see in fancy still,
Since ...

There now! Even for unthankful me,
Who stuck to my devotions at high-tide
That festal morning, never had a mind
To trudge the little league and join the crowd—
Even for me is miracle vouchsafed!
How pointless proves the sneer at miracles!

As if, contrariwise to all we want
And reasonably look to find, they graced
Merely those graced-before, grace helps no whit,
Unless, made whole, they need physician still.
I—sceptical in every inch of me—
Did I deserve that, from the liquid name
"Miranda,"—faceted as lovelily
As his own gift, the gem,—a shaft should shine,
Bear me along, another Abaris,
Nor let me light till, lo, the Red is reached,
And yonder lies in luminosity!

Look, lady! where I bade you glance but now!
Next habitation, though two miles away,—
No tenement for man or beast between,—
That, park and domicile, is country-seat
Of this same good Miranda! I accept
The augury. Or there, or nowhere else,
Will I establish that a Night-cap gleams
Of visionary Red, not White for once!
"Heaven," saith the sage, "is with us, here inside
Each man:" "Hell also," simpleness subjoins,
By White and Red describing human flesh.

And yet as we continue, quicken pace,
Approach the object which determines me
Victorious or defeated, more forlorn
My chance seems,—that is certainty at least.
Halt midway, reconnoitre! Either side
The path we traverse (turn and see) stretch fields
Without a hedge: one level, scallop-striped
With bands of beet and turnip and luzern,
Limited only by each color's end,
Shelves down—we stand upon an eminence—
To where the earth-shell scallops out the sea,
A sweep of semicircle; and at edge—
Just as the milk-white incrustations stud
At intervals some shell-extremity,
So do the little growths attract us here,
Towns with each name I told you: say, they touch
The sea, and the sea them, and all is said,
So sleeps and sets to slumber that broad blue!
The people are as peaceful as the place.
This, that I call "the path" is road, highway;
But has there passed us by a market-cart,
Man, woman, child, or dog to wag a tail?
True, I saw weeders stooping in a field;
But—formidably white the Cap's extent!

Round again! Come, appearance promises!
The boundary, the park-wall, ancient brick,
Upholds a second wall of tree-heads high
Which overlean its top, a solid green.
That surely ought to shut in mysteries!
A jeweller—no unsuggestive craft!
Trade that admits of much romance, indeed.
For, whom but goldsmiths used old monarchs pledge
Regalia to, or seek a ransom from,
Or pray to furnish dowry, at a pinch,
According to authentic story-books?
Why, such have revolutionized this land
With diamond-necklace-dealing! not to speak
Of families turned upside-down, because
The gay "wives went and pawned clandestinely
Jewels, and figured, till found out, with paste,
Or else redeemed them—how, is horrible!
Then there are those enormous criminals
That love their ware and cannot lose their love,
And murder you to get your purchase back.
Others go courting after such a stone,
Make it their mistress, marry for their wife,
And find out, some day, it was false the while,
As ever wife or mistress, man too fond
Has named his Pilgrim, Hermit, Ace of Hearts.

Beside—what style of edifice begins
To grow in sight at last and top the scene?
That gray roof, with the range of lucarnes, four
I count, and that erection in the midst—
Clock-house, or chapel-spire, or what, above?
Conventual, that, beyond, manorial, sure!
And reason good; for Clairvaux, such its name,
Was built of old to be a Priory,
Dependence on that Abbey-for-the-Males
Our Conqueror founded in world-famous Caen,
And where his body sought the sepulture,
It was not to retain: you know the tale.
Such Priory was Clairvaux, prosperous
Hundreds of years; but nothing lasts below,
And when the Red Cap pushed the Crown aside,
The Priory became, like all its peers,
A National Domain: which, bought and sold
And resold, needs must change, with ownership.
Both outside show and inside use; at length
The messuage, three-and-twenty years ago,
Became the purchase of rewarded worth

Impersonate in Father—I must stoop
To French phrase for precision's sake, I fear—
Father Miranda, goldsmith of renown:
By birth a Madrilene, by domicile
And sojourning accepted French at last.
His energy it was which, trade transferred
To Paris, throve as with a golden thumb,
Established in the Place Vendôme. He bought
Not building only, but belongings far
And wide, at Gonthier there, Monlieu, Villeneuve,
A plentiful estate: which, twelve years since,
Passed, at the good man's natural demise,
To Son and Heir Miranda—Clairvaux here,
The Paris shop, the mansion—not to say
Palatial residence on Quai Rousseau,
With money, movables, a mine of wealth—
And young Léonce Miranda got it all.

Ah, but—whose might the transformation be?
Were you prepared for this, now? As we talked,
We walked, we entered the half-privacy,
The partly-guarded precinct: passed beside
The little paled-off islet, trees and turf,
Then found us in the main ash-avenue
Under the blessing of its branchage-roof:
Till, on emergence, what affronts our gaze?
Priory—Conqueror—Abbey-for-the-Males—
Hey, presto, pass, who conjured all away?
Look through the railwork of the gate: a park
—Yes, but à l'Anglaise, as they compliment!
Grass like green velvet, gravel-walks like gold,
Bosses of shrubs, embosomings of flowers,
Lead you—through sprinkled trees of tiny breed
Disporting, within reach of coverture.
By some habitual acquiescent oak
Or elm, that thinks, and lets the youngsters laugh—
Lead, lift at last your soul that walks the air,
Up to the house-front, or its back perhaps—
Whether facade or no, one coquetry
Of colored brick and carved stone! Stucco? Well,
The daintiness is cheery, that I know,
And all the sportive floral framework fits
The lightsome purpose of the architect.
Those lucarnes which I called conventual, late,
Those are the outlets in the mansard-roof;
And, underneath, what long light elegance
Of windows here suggests how brave inside
Lurk eyeballed gems they play the eyelids to!

Festive arrangements look through such, be sure!
And now the tower a-top, I took for clock's
Or bell's abode, turns out a quaint device,
Pillared and temple-treated Belvedere—
Pavilion safe within its railed-about
Sublimity of area—whence what stretch,
Of sea and land, throughout the seasons' change,
Must greet the solitary! Or suppose,
—If what the husband likes, the wife likes too,—
The happy pair of students cloistered high,
Alone in April kiss when Spring arrives!
Or no, he mounts there by himself to meet
Winds, welcome wafts of sea-smell, first white bird
That flaps thus far to taste the land again,
And all the promise of the youthful year;
Then he descends, unbosoms straight his store
Of blessings in the bud, and both embrace,
Husband and wife, since earth is Paradise,
And man at peace with God. You see it all?

Let us complete our survey, go right round
The place: for here, it may be, we surprise
The Priory,—these solid walls, big barns,
Gray orchard-grounds, huge four-square stores for stock,
Betoken where the Church was busy once.
Soon must we come upon the Chapel's self.
No doubt next turn will treat us to ... Aha,
Again our expectation proves at fault!
Still the bright graceful modern—not to say
Modish adornment, meets us: Parc Anglais,
Tree-sprinkle, shrub-embossment as before.
See, the sun splits on yonder bauble world
Of silvered glass concentring, every side,
All the adjacent wonder, made minute
And touched grotesque by ball-convexity!
Just so, a sense that something is amiss,
Something is out of sorts in the display,
Affects us, past denial, everywhere.
The right erection for the Fields, the Wood,
(Fields—but Elysées, wood—but de Boulogne)
Is peradventure wrong for wood and fields
When Vire, not Paris, plays the Capital.
So may a good man have deficient taste;
Since Son and Heir Miranda, he it was
Who, six years now elapsed, achieved the work
And truly made a wilderness to smile.
Here did their domesticity reside,
A happy husband and as happy wife,

Till ... how can I in conscience longer keep
My little secret that the man is dead
I, for artistic purpose, talk about
As if he lived still? No, these two years now
Has he been dead. You ought to sympathize,
Not mock the sturdy effort to redeem
My pledge, and wring you out some tragedy
From even such a perfect commonplace!
Suppose I boast the death of such desert
My tragic bit of Red? Who contravenes
Assertion that a tragedy exists
In any stoppage of benevolence,
Utility, devotion above all?
Benevolent? There never was his like:
For poverty, he had an open hand
... Or stop—I use the wrong expression here—
An open purse, then, ever at appeal;
So that the unreflecting rather taxed
Profusion than penuriousness in alms.
One, in his day and generation, deemed
Of use to the community? I trust,
Clairvaux thus renovated, regalized,
Paris expounded thus to Normandy,
Answers that question. Was the man devout?
After a life—one mere munificence
To Church and all things churchly, men or mice,—
Dying, his last bequeathment gave land, goods,
Cash, every stick and stiver, to the Church,
And notably to that church yonder, that
Beloved of his soul, La Ravissante—
Wherefrom, the latest of his gifts, the Stone
Gratefully bore me as on arrow-flash
To Clairvaux, as I told you.

"Ay, to find
Your Red desiderated article,
Where every scratch and scrape provokes my White
To all the more superb a prominence!
Why, 't is the story served up fresh again—
How it befell the restive prophet old
Who came and tried to curse but blessed the land.
Come, your last chance! he disinherited
Children: he made his widow mourn too much
By this endowment of the other Bride—
Nor understood that gold and jewelry
Adorn her in a figure, not a fact.
You make that White I want, so very white,
'T is I say now—some trace of Red should be

Somewhere in this Miranda-sanctitude!"

Not here, at all events, sweet mocking friend!
For he was childless; and what heirs he had
Were an uncertain sort of Cousinry
Scarce claiming kindred so as to withhold
The donor's purpose though fantastical:
Heirs, for that matter, wanting no increase
Of wealth, since rich already as himself;
Heirs that had taken trouble off his hands,
Bought that productive goldsmith-business he,
With abnegation wise as rare, renounced
Precisely at a time of life when youth,
Nigh on departure, bids mid-age discard
Life's other loves and likings in a pack,
To keep, in lucre, comfort worth them all.
This Cousinry are they who boast the shop
Of "Firm-Miranda, London and New York."
Cousins are an unconscionable kind;
But these—pretension surely on their part
To share inheritance were too absurd!

"Remains then, he dealt wrongly by his wife,
Despoiled her somehow by such testament?"
Farther than ever from the mark, fair friend!
The man's love for his wife exceeded bounds
Rather than failed the limit. 'T was to live
Hers and hers only, to abolish earth
Outside—since Paris holds the pick of earth—
He turned his back, shut eyes, stopped ears, to all
Delicious Paris tempts her children with,
And fled away to this far solitude—
She peopling solitude sufficiently!
She, partner in each heavenward flight sublime,
Was, with each condescension to the ground,
Duly associate also: hand in hand,
... Or side by side, I say by preference—
On every good work sidlingly they went.
Hers was the instigation—none but she
Willed that, if death should summon first her lord,
Though she, sad relict, must drag residue
Of days encumbered by this load of wealth—
(Submitted to with something of a grace
So long as her surviving vigilance
Might worthily administer, convert
Wealth to God's glory and the good of man,
Give, as in life, so now in death, effect
To cherished purpose)—yet she begged and prayed

That, when no longer she could supervise
The House, it should become a Hospital:
For the support whereof, lands, goods, and cash
Alike will go, in happy guardianship,
To yonder church, La Ravissante: who debt
To God and man undoubtedly will pay.

"Not of the world, your heroine!"

Do you know
I saw her yesterday—set eyes upon
The veritable personage, no dream?
I in the morning strolled this way, as oft,
And stood at entry of the avenue.
When, out from that first garden-gate, we gazed
Upon and through, a small procession swept—
Madame Miranda with attendants five.
First, of herself: she wore a soft and white
Engaging dress, with velvet stripes and squares
Severely black, yet scarce discouraging:
Fresh Paris-manufacture! (Vire's would do?
I doubt it, but confess my ignorance.)
Her figure? somewhat small and darling-like.
Her face? well, singularly colorless,
For first thing: which scarce suits a blonde, you know.
Pretty you would not call her: though perhaps
Attaining to the ends of prettiness,
And somewhat more, suppose enough of soul.
Then she is forty full: you cannot judge
What beauty was her portion at eighteen,
The age she married at. So, colorless
I stick to, and if featureless I add,
Your notion grows completer: for, although
I noticed that her nose was aquiline,
The whole effect amounts with me to—blank!
I never saw what I could less describe.
The eyes, for instance, unforgettable
Which ought to be, are out of mind as sight.

Yet is there not conceivably a face,
A set of wax-like features, blank at first,
Which, as you bendingly grow warm above,
Begins to take impressment from your breath?
Which, as your will itself were plastic here
Nor needed exercise of handicraft,
From formless moulds itself to correspond
With all you think and feel and are—in fine
Grows a new revelation of yourself,

Who know now for the first time what you want?
Here has been something that could wait awhile,
Learn your requirement, nor take shape before,
But, by adopting it, make palpable
Your right to an importance of your own,
Companions somehow were so slow to see!
—Far delicater solace to conceit
Than should some absolute and final face,
Fit representative of soul inside,
Summon you to surrender—in no way
Your breath's impressment, nor, in stranger's guise,
Yourself—or why of force to challenge you?
Why should your soul's reflection rule your soul?
("You" means not you, nor me, nor any one
Framed, for a reason I shall keep suppressed,
To rather want a master than a slave:
The slavish still aspires to dominate!)
So, all I say is, that the face, to me
One blur of blank, might flash significance
To who had seen his soul reflected there
By that symmetric silvery phantom-like
Figure, with other five processional.
The first, a black-dressed matron—maybe, maid—
Mature, and dragonish of aspect,—marched;
Then four came tripping in a joyous flock,
Two giant goats and two prodigious sheep
Pure as the arctic fox that suits the snow,
Tripped, trotted, turned the march to merriment,
But ambled at their mistress' heel—for why?
A rod of guidance marked the Châtelaine,
And ever and anon would sceptre wave,
And silky subject leave meandering.
Nay, one great naked sheep-face stopped to ask
Who was the stranger, snuffed inquisitive
My hand that made acquaintance with its nose,
Examined why the hand—of man at least—
Patted so lightly, warmly, so like life!
Are they such silly natures after all?
And thus accompanied, the paled-off space,
Isleted shrubs and verdure, gained the group;
Till, as I gave a furtive glance, and saw
Her back-hair was a block of solid gold,
The gate shut out my harmless question—Hair
So young and yellow, crowning sanctity,
And claiming solitude ... can hair be false?

"Shut in the hair and with it your last hope,
Yellow might on inspection pass for Red!—

Red, Red, where is the tinge of promised Red
In this old tale of town and country life,
This rise and progress of a family?
First comes the bustling man of enterprise,
The fortune-founding father, rightly rough,
As who must grub and grab, play pioneer.
Then, with a light and airy step, succeeds
The son, surveys the fabric of his sire,
And enters home, unsmirched from top to toe.
Polish and education qualify
Their fortunate possessor to confine
His occupancy to the first-floor suite
Rather than keep exploring needlessly
Where dwelt his sire content with cellarage:
Industry bustles underneath, no doubt,
And supervisors should not sit too close.
Next, rooms built, there 's the furniture to buy,
And what adornment like a worthy wife?
In comes she like some foreign cabinet,
Purchased indeed, but purifying quick
What space receives it from all traffic-taint.
She tells of other habits, palace-life;
Royalty may have pried into those depths
Of sandal-wooded drawer, and set a-creak
That pygmy portal pranked with lazuli.
More fit by far the ignoble we replace
By objects suited to such visitant,
Than that we desecrate her dignity
By neighborhood of vulgar table, chair,
Which haply helped old age to smoke and doze.
The end is, an exchange of city stir
And too intrusive burgess-fellowship,
For rural isolated elegance,
Careless simplicity, how preferable!
There one may fairly throw behind one's back
The used-up worn-out Past, we want away,
And make a fresh beginning of stale life.
'In just the place'—does any one object?—
'Where aboriginal gentility
Will scout the upstart, twit him with each trick
Of townish trade-mark that stamps word and deed,
And most of all resent that here town-dross
He daubs with money-color to deceive!'
Rashly objected! Is there not the Church
To intercede and bring benefic truce
At outset? She it is shall equalize
The laborers i' the vineyard, last as first.
Pay court to her, she stops impertinence.

'Duke, once your sires crusaded it, we know:
Our friend the newcomer observes, no less,
Your chapel, rich with their emblazonry,
Wants roofing—might he but supply the means!
Marquise, you gave the honor of your name,
Titular patronage, abundant will
To what should be an Orphan Institute:
Gave everything but funds, in brief; and these,
Our friend, the lady newly resident,
Proposes to contribute, by your leave!'
Brothers and sisters lie they in thy lap,
Thou none-excluding, all-collecting Church!
Sure, one has half a foot i' the hierarchy
Of birth, when 'Nay, my dear,' laughs out the Duke,
'I 'm the crown's cushion-carrier, but the crown—
Who gave its central glory, I or you?'
When Marquise jokes, 'My quest, forsooth? Each doit
I scrape together goes for Peter-pence
To purvey bread and water in his bonds
For Peter's self imprisoned—Lord, how long?
Yours, yours alone the bounty, dear my dame,
You plumped the purse, which, poured into the plate,
Made the Archbishop open brows so broad!
And if you really mean to give that length
Of lovely lace to edge the robe!' ... Ah, friends,
Gem better serves so than by calling crowd,
Round shop-front to admire the million's-worth!
Lace gets more homage than from lorgnette-stare,
And comment coarse to match, (should one display
One's robe a trifle o'er the baignoire-edge,)
'Well may she line her slippers with the like,
If minded so! their shop it was produced
That wonderful parure, the other day,
Whereof the Baron said, it beggared him.'
And so the paired Mirandas built their house,
Enjoyed their fortune, sighed for family,
Found friends would serve their purpose quite as well,
And come, at need, from Paris—anyhow,
With evident alacrity, from Vire—
Endeavor at the chase, at least succeed
In smoking, eating, drinking, laughing, and
Preferring country, oh so much to town!
Thus lived the husband; though his wife would sigh
In confidence, when Countesses were kind,
'Cut off from Paris and society!'
White, White, I once more round you in the ears!
Though you have marked it, in a corner, yours
Henceforth,—Red-lettered 'Failure,' very plain,

I shall acknowledge, on the snowy hem
Of ordinary Night-cap! Come, enough!
We have gone round its cotton vastitude,
Or half-round, for the end 's consistent still,
A cul-de-sac with stoppage at the sea.
Here we return upon our steps. One look
May bid good-morning—properly good-night—
To civic bliss, Miranda and his mate!
Are we to rise and go?"

No, sit and stay!
Now comes my moment, with the thrilling throw
Of curtain from each side a shrouded case.
Don't the rings shriek an ominous "Ha! ha!
So you take Human Nature upon trust"?
List but with like trust to an incident
Which speedily shall make quite Red enough
Burn out of yonder spotless napery!
Sit on the little mound here, whence you seize
The whole of the gay front sun-satisfied,
One laugh of color and embellishment!
Because it was there,—past those laurustines,
On that smooth gravel-sweep 'twixt flowers and sward,—
There tragic death befell; and not one grace
Outspread before you but is registered
In that sinistrous coil these last two years
Were occupied in winding smooth again.

"True?" Well, at least it was concluded so,
Sworn to be truth, allowed by Law as such,
(With my concurrence, if it matter here,)
A month ago: at Vire they tried the case.

II

Monsieur Léonce Miranda, then, ... but stay!
Permit me a preliminary word,
And, after, all shall go so straight to end!

Have you, the travelled lady, found yourself
Inside a ruin, fane or bath or cirque,
Renowned in story, dear through youthful dream?
If not,—imagination serves as well.
Try fancy-land, go back a thousand years,
Or forward, half the number, and confront
Some work of art gnawn hollow by Time's tooth,—
Hellenic temple, Roman theatre,

Gothic cathedral, Gallic Tuileries,
But ruined, one and whichsoe'er you like.
Obstructions choke what still remains intact,
Yet proffer change that 's picturesque in turn;
Since little life begins where great life ends,
And vegetation soon amalgamates,
Smooths novel shape from out the shapeless old,
Till broken column, battered cornice-block,
The centre with a bulk half weeds and flowers,
Half relics you devoutly recognize.
Devoutly recognizing,—hark, a voice
Not to be disregarded! "Man worked here
Once on a time; here needs again to work;
Ruins obstruct, which man must remedy."
Would you demur "Let Time fulfil his task,
And, till the scythe-sweep find no obstacle,
Let man be patient"?

The reply were prompt:
"Glisteningly beneath the May-night moon,
Herbage and floral coverture bedeck
Yon splintered mass amidst the solitude:
Wolves occupy the background, or some snake
Glides by at distance: picturesque enough?
Therefore, preserve it? Nay, pour daylight in,—
The mound proves swarming with humanity.
There never was a thorough solitude,
Now you look nearer: mortal busy life
First of all brought the crumblings down on pate,
Which trip man's foot still, plague his passage much,
And prove—what seems to you so picturesque
To him is ... but experiment yourself
On how conducive to a happy home
Will be the circumstance, your bed for base
Boasts tessellated pavement,—equally
Affected by the scorpion for his nest,—
While what o'er-roofs bed is an architrave,
Marble, and not unlikely to crush man
To mummy, should its venerable prop,
Some figtree-stump, play traitor underneath.
Be wise! Decide! For conservation's sake,
Clear the arena forthwith! lest the tread
Of too-much-tried impatience trample out
Solid and unsubstantial to one blank
Mud-mixture, picturesque to nobody,—
And, task done, quarrel with the parts intact
Whence came the filtered fine dust, whence the crash
Bides but its time to follow. Quick conclude

Removal, time effects so tardily,
Of what is plain obstruction; rubbish cleared,
Let partial-ruin stand while ruin may,
And serve world's use, since use is manifold.
Repair wreck, stanchion wall to heart's content,
But never think of renovation pure
And simple, which involves creation too:
Transform and welcome! Yon tall tower may help
(Though built to be a belfry and naught else)
Some Father Secchi, to tick Venus off
In transit: never bring there bell again,
To damage him aloft, brain us below,
When new vibrations bury both in brick!"

Monsieur Léonce Miranda, furnishing
The application at his cost, poor soul!
Was instanced how,—because the world lay strewn
With ravage of opinions in his path,
And neither he, nor any friendly wit,
Knew and could teach him which was firm, which frail,
In his adventure to walk straight through life
The partial-ruin,—in such enterprise,
He straggled into rubbish, struggled on,
And stumbled out again observably.
"Yon buttress still can back me up," he judged:
And at a touch down came both he and it.
"A certain statue, I was warned against,
Now, by good fortune, lies well underfoot,
And cannot tempt to folly any more:"
So, lifting eye, aloft since safety lay,
What did he light on? the Idalian shape,
The undeposed, erectly Victrix still!
"These steps ascend the labyrinthine stair
Whence, darkling and on all-fours, out I stand
Exalt and safe, and bid low earth adieu—
For so instructs 'Advice to who would climb:'"
And all at once the climbing landed him
—Where, is my story.

Take its moral first.
Do you advise a climber? Have respect
To the poor head, with more or less of brains
To spill, should breakage follow your advice!
Head-break to him will be heart-break to you
For having preached "Disturb no ruins here!
Are not they crumbling of their own accord?
Meantime, let poets, painters keep a prize!
Beside, a sage pedestrian picks his way."

A sage pedestrian—such as you and I!
What if there trip, in merry carelessness,
And come to grief, a weak and foolish child?
Be cautious how you counsel climbing, then!

Are you adventurous and climb yourself?
Plant the foot warily, accept a staff,
Stamp only where you probe the standing-point,
Move forward, well assured that move you may:
Where you mistrust advance, stop short, there stick!
This makes advancing slow and difficult?
Hear what comes of the endeavor of brisk youth
To foot it fast and easy! Keep this same
Notion of outside mound and inside mash,
Towers yet intact round turfy rottenness,
Symbolic partial-ravage,—keep in mind!
Here fortune placed his feet who first of all
Found no incumbrance, till head found ... But hear!

This son and heir then of the jeweller,
Monsieur Léonce Miranda, at his birth,
Mixed the Castilian passionate blind blood
With answerable gush, his mother's gift,
Of spirit, French and critical and cold.
Such mixture makes a battle in the brain,
Ending as faith or doubt gets uppermost;
Then will has way a moment, but no more:
So nicely balanced are the adverse strengths,
That victory entails reverse next time.
The tactics of the two are different
And equalize the odds: for blood comes first,
Surrounding life with undisputed faith.
But presently a new antagonist,
By scarce-suspected passage in the dark,
Steals spirit, fingers at each crevice found
Athwart faith's stronghold, fronts the astonished man:
"Such pains to keep me far, yet here stand I,
Your doubt inside the faith-defence of you!"

With faith it was friends bulwarked him about
From infancy to boyhood; so, by youth,
He stood impenetrably circuited,
Heaven-high and low as hell: what lacked he thus,
Guarded against aggression, storm or sap?
What foe would dare approach? Historic Doubt?
Ay, were there some half-knowledge to attack!
Batter doubt's best, sheer ignorance will beat.
Acumen metaphysic?—drills its way

Through what, I wonder! A thick feather-bed
Of thoughtlessness, no operating tool—
Framed to transpierce the flint-stone—fumbles at,
With chance of finding an impediment!
This Ravissante, now: when he saw the church
For the first time, and to his dying-day,
His firm belief was that the name fell fit
From the Delivering Virgin, niched and known;
As if there wanted records to attest
The appellation was a pleasantry,
A pious rendering of Rare Vissante,
The proper name which erst our province bore.
He would have told you that Saint Aldabert
Founded the church, (Heaven early favored France,)
About the second century from Christ;
Though the true man was Bishop of Raimbaux,
Eleventh in succession, Eldobert,
Who flourished after some six hundred years.
He it was brought the image "from afar,"
(Made out of stone the place produces still,)
"Infantine Art divinely artless," (Art
In the decrepitude of Decadence,)
And set it up a-working miracles
Until the Northmen's fury laid it low,
Not long, however: an egregious sheep,
Zealous with scratching hoof and routing horn,
Unearthed the image in good Mailleville's time,
Count of the country. "If the tale be false,
Why stands it carved above the portal plain?"
Monsieur Léonce Miranda used to ask.
To Londres went the prize in solemn pomp,
But, liking old abode and loathing new,
Was borne—this time, by angels—back again.
And, reinaugurated, miracle
Succeeded miracle, a lengthy list,
Until indeed the culmination came—
Archbishop Chaumont prayed a prayer and vowed
A vow—gained prayer and paid vow properly—
For the conversion of Prince Vertgalant.
These facts, sucked in along with mother's-milk,
Monsieur Léonce Miranda would dispute
As soon as that his hands were flesh and bone,
Milk-nourished two-and-twenty years before.
So fortified by blind Castilian blood,
What say you to the chances of French cold
Critical spirit, should Voltaire besiege
"Alp, Apennine, and fortified redoubt"?
Ay, would such spirit please to play faith's game

Faith's way, attack where faith defends so well!
But then it shifts, tries other strategy.
Coldness grows warmth, the critical becomes
Unquestioning acceptance. "Share and share
Alike in facts, to truth add other truth!
Why with old truth needs new truth disagree?"

Thus doubt was found invading faith, this time,
By help of not the spirit but the flesh:
Fat Rabelais chuckled, where faith lay in wait
For lean Voltaire's grimace—French, either foe.
Accordingly, while round about our friend
Ran faith without a break which learned eye
Could find at two-and-twenty years of age,
The twenty-two-years-old frank footstep soon
Assured itself there spread a standing-space
Flowery and comfortable, nowise rock
Nor pebble-pavement roughed for champion's tread
Who scorns discomfort, pacing at his post.
Tall, long-limbed, shoulder right and shoulder left,
And 'twixt acromia such a latitude,
Black heaps of hair on head, and blacker bush
O'er-rioting chin, cheek and throat and chest,—
His brown meridional temperament
Told him—or rather pricked into his sense
Plainer than language—"Pleasant station here!
Youth, strength, and lustihood can sleep on turf
Yet pace the stony platform afterward:
First signal of a foe and up they start!
Saint Eldobert, at all such vanity,
Nay—sinfulness, had shaken head austere.
Had he? But did Prince Vertgalant? And yet,
After how long a slumber, of what sort,
Was it, he stretched octogenary joints,
And, nigh on Day-of-Judgment trumpet-blast,
Jumped up and manned wall, brisk as any bee?"

Nor Rabelais nor Voltaire, but Sganarelle,
You comprehend, was pushing through the chink!
That stager in the saint's correct costume,
Who ever has his speech in readiness
For thick-head juvenility at fault:
"Go pace yon platform and play sentinel!
You won't? The worse! but still a worse might hap.
Stay then, provided that you keep in sight
The battlement, one bold leap lands you by!
Resolve not desperately 'Wall or turf,
Choose this, choose that, but no alternative!

No! Earth left once were left for good and all:
'With Heaven you may accommodate yourself.'"

Saint Eldobert—I much approve his mode;
With sinner Vertgalant I sympathize;
But histrionic Sganarelle, who prompts
While pulling back, refuses yet concedes,—
Whether he preach in chair, or print in book,
Or whisper due sustainment to weak flesh,
Counting his sham beads threaded on a lie—
Surely, one should bid pack that mountebank!
Surely, he must have momentary fits
Of self-sufficient stage-forgetfulness,
Escapings of the actor-lassitude
When he allows the grace to show the grin,
Which ought to let even thickheads recognize
(Through all the busy and benefic part,—
Bridge-building, or rock-riving, or good clean
Transport of church and congregation both
From this to that place with no harm at all,)
The Devil, that old stager, at his trick
Of general utility, who leads
Downward, perhaps, but fiddles all the way!

Therefore, no sooner does our candidate
For saintship spotlessly emerge soul-cleansed
From First Communion to mount guard at post,
Paris-proof, top to toe, than up there start
The Spirit of the Boulevard—you know Who—
With jocund "So, a structure fixed as fate,
Faith's tower joins on to tower, no ring more round,
Full fifty years at distance, too, from youth!
Once reach that precinct and there fight your best,
As looking back you wonder what has come
Of daisy-dappled turf you danced across!
Few flowers that played with youth shall pester age,
However age esteem the courtesy;
And Eldobert was something past his prime,
Stocked Caen with churches ere he tried hand here.
Saint-Sauveur, Notre-Dame, Saint-Pierre, Saint-Jean
Attest his handiwork commenced betimes.
He probably would preach that turf is mud.
Suppose it mud, through mud one picks a way,
And when, clay-clogged, the struggler steps to stone,
He uncakes shoe, arrives in manlier guise
Than carried pick-a-back by Eldobert
Big-baby-fashion, lest his leathers leak!
All that parade about Prince Vertgalant

Amounts to—your Castilian helps enough—
Inveni ovem quæ perierat.
But ask the pretty votive statue-thing
What the lost sheep's meantime amusements were
Till the Archbishop found him! That stays blank:
They washed the fleece well and forgot the rest.
Make haste, since time flies, to determine, though!"

Thus opportunely took up parable,—
Admonishing Miranda just emerged
Pure from The Ravissante and Paris-proof,—
Saint Sganarelle: then slipped aside, changed mask,
And made re-entry as a gentleman
Born of the Boulevard, with another speech,
I spare you.

So, the year or two revolved,
And ever the young man was dutiful
To altar and to hearth: had confidence
In the whole Ravissantish history.
Voltaire? Who ought to know so much of him,—
Old sciolist, whom only boys think sage,—
As one whose father's house upon the Quai
Neighbored the very house where that Voltaire
Died mad and raving, not without a burst
Of squibs and crackers too significant?
Father and mother hailed their best of sons,
Type of obedience, domesticity,
Never such an example inside doors!
Outside, as well not keep too close a watch;
Youth must be left to some discretion there.
And what discretion proved, I find deposed
At Vire, confirmed by his own words: to wit,
How, with the spriteliness of twenty-five,
Five—and not twenty, for he gave their names
With laudable precision—were the few
Appointed by him unto mistress-ship;
While, meritoriously the whole long week
A votary of commerce only, week
Ended, "at shut of shop on Saturday,
Do I, as is my wont, get drunk," he writes
In airy record to a confidant.
"Bragging and lies!" replies the apologist:
"And do I lose by that?" laughed Somebody,
At the Court-edge a-tiptoe, 'mid the crowd,
In his own clothes, a-listening to men's Law.

Thus while, prospectively a combatant,

The volunteer bent brows, clenched jaws, and fierce
Whistled the march-tune "Warrior to the wall!"
Something like flowery laughters round his feet
Tangled him of a sudden with "Sleep first!"
And fairly flat upon the turf sprawled he,
And let strange creatures make his mouth their home.

Anyhow, 't is the nature of the soul
To seek a show of durability,
Nor, changing, plainly be the slave of change.
Outside the turf, the towers: but, round the turf,
A tent may rise, a temporary shroud,
Mock-faith to suit a mimic dwelling-place:
Tent which, while screening jollity inside
From the external circuit—evermore
A menace to who lags when he should march—
Yet stands a-tremble, ready to collapse
At touch of foot: turf is acknowledged grass,
And grass, though pillowy, held contemptible
Compared with solid rock, the rampired ridge.
To truth a pretty homage thus we pay
By testifying—what we dally with,
Falsehood, (which, never fear we take for truth!)
We may enjoy, but then—how we despise!

Accordingly, on weighty business bound,
Monsieur Léonce Miranda stooped to play,
But, with experience, soon reduced the game
To principles, and thenceforth played by rule:
Rule, dignifying sport as sport, proclaimed
No less that sport was sport, and nothing more.
He understood the worth of womankind,—
To furnish man—provisionally—sport:
Sport transitive—such earth's amusements are:
But, seeing that amusements pall by use,
Variety therein is requisite.
And since the serious work of life were wronged
Should we bestow importance on our play,
It follows, in such womankind-pursuit,
Cheating is lawful chase. We have to spend
An hour—they want a lifetime thrown away:
We seek to tickle sense—they ask for soul,
As if soul had no higher ends to serve!
A stag-hunt gives the royal creature law:
Bat-fowling is all fair with birds at roost,
The lantern and the clap-net suit the hedge.
Which must explain why, bent on Boulevard game,
Monsieur Léonce Miranda decently

Was prudent in his pleasure—passed himself
Off on the fragile fair about his path
As the gay devil rich in mere good looks,
Youth, hope—what matter though the purse be void?
"If I were only young Miranda, now,
Instead of a poor clerkly drudge at desk
All day, poor artist vainly bruising brush
On palette, poor musician scraping gut
With horsehair teased that no harmonics come!
Then would I love with liberality,
Then would I pay!—who now shall be repaid,
Repaid alike for present pain and past,
If Mademoiselle permit the contre-danse,
Sing 'Gay in garret youth at twenty lives,'
And afterward accept a lemonade!"

Such sweet facilities of intercourse
Afford the Winter-Garden and Mabille!
"Oh, I unite"—runs on the confidence,
Poor fellow, that was read in open Court,
—"Amusement with discretion: never fear
My escapades cost more than market-price!
No durably-attached Miranda-dupe,
Sucked dry of substance by two clinging lips,
Promising marriage, and performing it!
Trust me, I know the world, and know myself,
And know where duty takes me—in good time!"

Thus fortified and realistic, then,
At all points thus against illusion armed,
He wisely did New Year inaugurate
By playing truant to the favored five:
And sat installed at "The Varieties,"—
Playhouse appropriately named,—to note
(Prying amid the turf that 's flowery there)
What primrose, firstling of the year, might push
The snows aside to deck his buttonhole—
Unnoticed by that outline sad, severe,
(Though fifty good long years removed from youth,)
That tower and tower,—our image bear in mind!

No sooner was he seated than, behold,
Out burst a polyanthus! He was 'ware
Of a young woman niched in neighborhood;
And ere one moment flitted, fast was he
Found captive to the beauty evermore,
For life, for death, for heaven, for hell, her own.
Philosophy, bewail thy fate! Adieu,

Youth realistic and illusion-proof!
Monsieur Léonce Miranda,—hero late
Who "understood the worth of womankind,"
"Who found therein—provisionally—sport,"—
Felt, in the flitting of a moment, fool
Was he, and folly all that seemed so wise,
And the best proof of wisdom's birth would be
That he made all endeavor, body, soul,
By any means, at any sacrifice
Of labor, wealth, repute, and (—well, the time
For choosing between heaven on earth, and heaven
In heaven, was not at hand immediately—)
Made all endeavor, without loss incurred
Of one least minute, to obtain her love.
"Sport transitive?" "Variety required?"
"In loving were a lifetime thrown away?"
How singularly may young men mistake!
The fault must be repaired with energy.
Monsieur Léonce Miranda ate her up
With eye-devouring; when the unconscious fair
Passed from the close-packed hall, he pressed behind;
She mounted vehicle, he did the same,
Coach stopped, and cab fast followed, at one door—
Good house in unexceptionable street.
Out stepped the lady,—never think, alone!
A mother was not wanting to the maid,
Or, maybe, wife, or widow, might one say?
Out stepped and properly down flung himself
Monsieur Léonce Miranda at her feet—
And never left them after, so to speak,
For twenty years, till his last hour of life,
When he released them, as precipitate.
Love proffered and accepted then and there!
Such potency in word and look has truth.

Truth I say, truth I mean: this love was true,
And the rest happened by due consequence.
By which we are to learn that there exists
A falsish false, for truth 's inside the same,
And truth that 's only half true, falsish truth.
The better for both parties! folks may taunt
That half your rock-built wall is rubble-heap:
Answer them, half their flowery turf is stones!
Our friend had hitherto been decking coat
If not with stones, with weeds that stones befit,
With dandelions—"primrose-buds," smirked he;
This proved a polyanthus on his breast,
Prize-lawful or prize-lawless, flower the same.

So with his other instance of mistake:
Was Christianity the Ravissante?

And what a flower of flowers he chanced on now!
To primrose, polyanthus I prefer
As illustration, from the fancy-fact
That out of simple came the composite
By culture: that the florist bedded thick
His primrose-root in ruddle, bullock's blood,
Ochre and devils'-dung, for aught I know,
Until the pale and pure grew fiery-fine,
Ruby and topaz, rightly named anew.
This lady was no product of the plain;
Social manure had raised a rarity.
Clara de Millefleurs (note the happy name)
Blazed in the full-blown glory of her Spring.
Peerlessly perfect, form and face: for both—
"Imagine what, at seventeen, may have proved
Miss Pages, the actress: Pages herself, my dear!"
Noble she was, the name denotes: and rich?
"The apartment in this Coliseum Street,
Furnished, my dear, with such an elegance,
Testifies wealth, my dear, sufficiently!
What quality, what style and title, eh?
Well now, waive nonsense, you and I are boys
No longer: somewhere must a screw be slack!
Don't fancy, Duchesses descend at door
From carriage-step to stranger prostrate stretched,
And bid him take heart, and deliver mind,
March in and make himself at ease forthwith,—
However broad his chest and black his beard,
And comely his belongings,—all through love
Protested in a world of ways save one—
Hinting at marriage!"—marriage which yet means
Only the obvious method, easiest help
To satisfaction of love's first demand,
That love endure eternally: "my dear,
Somewhere or other must a screw be slack!"

Truth is the proper policy: from truth—
Whate'er the force wherewith you fling your speech,—
Be sure that speech will lift you, by rebound,
Somewhere above the lowness of a lie!
Monsieur Léonce Miranda heard too true
A tale—perhaps I may subjoin, too trite!
As the meek martyr takes her statued stand
Above our pity, claims our worship just
Because of what she puts in evidence,

Signal of suffering, badge of torture borne
In days gone by, shame then, but glory now,
Barb, in the breast, turned aureole for the front!
So, half timidity, composure half,
Clara de Millefleurs told her martyrdom.

Of poor though noble parentage, deprived
Too early of a father's guardianship,
What wonder if the prodigality
Of nature in the girl, whose mental gifts
Matched her external dowry, form and face—
If these suggested a too prompt resource
To the resourceless mother? "Try the Stage,
And so escape starvation! Prejudice
Defames Mimetic Art: be yours to prove
That gold and dross may meet and never mix,
Purity plunge in pitch yet soil no plume!"

All was prepared in London—(you conceive
The natural shrinking from publicity
In Paris, where the name excites remark)—
London was ready for the grand début;
When some perverse ill-fortune, incident
To art mimetic, some malicious thrust
Of Jealousy who sidles 'twixt the scenes,
Or pops up sudden from the prompter's hole,—
Somehow the brilliant bubble burst in suds.
Want followed: in a foreign land, the pair!
Oh, hurry over the catastrophe—
Mother too sorely tempted, daughter tried
Scarcely so much as circumvented, say!
Caged unsuspecting artless innocence!

Monsieur Léonce Miranda tell the rest!—
The rather that he told it in a style
To puzzle Court Guide students, much more me.
"Brief, she became the favorite of Lord N.,
An aged but illustrious Duke, thereby
Breaking the heart of his competitor,
The Prince of O. Behold her palaced straight
In splendor, clothed in diamonds," (phrase how fit!)
"Giving tone to the City by the Thames!
Lord N., the aged but illustrious Duke,
Was even on the point of wedding her—
Giving his name to her" (why not to us?)
"But that her better angel interposed.
She fled from such a fate to Paris back.
A fortnight since: conceive Lord N.'s despair!

Duke as he is, there 's no invading France.
He must restrict pursuit to postal plague
Of writing letters daily, duly read
As darlingly she hands them to myself,
The privileged supplanter, who therewith
Light a cigar and see abundant blue"—
(Either of heaven or else Havana-smoke,)
"Think! she, who helped herself to diamonds late,
In passion of disinterestedness
Now—will accept no tribute of my love
Beyond a paltry ring, three Louis'-worth!
Little she knows I have the rummaging
Of old Papa's shop in the Place Vendôme!"
So wrote entrancedly to confidant,
Monsieur Léonce Miranda. Surely now,
If Heaven, that see all, understands no less,
It finds temptation pardonable here,
It mitigates the promised punishment,
It recognizes that to tarry just
An April hour amid such dainty turf
Means no rebellion against task imposed
Of journey to the distant wall one day?
Monsieur Léonce Miranda puts the case!
Love, he is purposed to renounce, abjure;
But meanwhile, is the case a common one?
Is it the vulgar sin, none hates as he?
Which question, put directly to "his dear"
(His brother—I will tell you in a trice),
Was doubtless meant, by due meandering,
To reach, to fall not unobserved before
The auditory cavern 'neath the cope
Of Her, the placable, the Ravissante.
But here 's the drawback, that the image smiles,
Smiles on, smiles ever, says to supplicant
"Ay, ay, ay"—like some kindly weathercock
Which, stuck fast at Set Fair, Favonian Breeze,
Still warrants you from rain, though Auster's lead
Bring down the sky above your cloakless mirth.
Had he proposed this question to, nor "dear"
Nor Ravissante, but prompt to the Police,
The Commissary of his Quarter, now—
There had been shaggy eyebrows elevate
With twinkling apprehension in each orb
Beneath, and when the sudden shut of mouth
Relaxed,—lip pressing lip, lest out should plump
The pride of knowledge in too frank a flow,—
Then, fact on fact forthcoming, dose were dealt
Of truth remedial, in sufficiency

To save a chicken threatened with the pip,
Head-staggers and a tumble from its perch.

Alack, it was the lady's self that made
The revelation, after certain days
—Nor so unwisely! As the haschisch-man
Prepares a novice to receive his drug,
Adroitly hides the soil with sudden spread
Of carpet ere he seats his customer:
Then shows him how to smoke himself about
With Paradise; and only when, at puff
Of pipe, the Houri dances round the brain
Of dreamer, does he judge no need is now
For circumspection and punctiliousness;
He may resume the serviceable scrap
That made the votary unaware of muck.
Just thus the lady, when her brewage—love—
Was well a-fume about the novice-brain,
Saw she might boldly pluck from underneath
Her lover the preliminary lie.

Clara de Millefleurs, of the noble race,
Was Lucie Steiner, child to Dominique
And Magdalen Commercy; born at Sierck,
About the bottom of the Social Couch.
The father having come and gone again,
The mother and the daughter found their way
To Paris, and professed mode-merchandise,
Were milliners, we English roughlier say;
And soon a fellow-lodger in the house,
Monsieur Ulysse Muhlhausen, young and smart,
Tailor by trade, perceived his house-mate's youth,
Smartness, and beauty over and above.
Courtship was brief, and marriage followed quick,
And quicklier—impecuniosity.
The young pair quitted Paris to reside
At London: which repaid the compliment
But scurvily, since not a whit the more
Trade prospered by the Thames than by the Seine.
Failing all other, as a last resource,
"He would have trafficked in his wife,"—she said.
If for that cause they quarrelled, 't was, I fear,
Rather from reclamation of her rights
To wifely independence, than as wronged
Otherwise by the course of life proposed:
Since, on escape to Paris back again,
From horror and the husband,—ill-exchanged
For safe maternal home recovered thus,—

I find her domiciled and dominant
In that apartment, Coliseum Street,
Where all the splendid magic met and mazed
Monsieur Léonce Miranda's venturous eye.
Only, the same was furnished at the cost
Of some one notable in days long since,
Carlino Centofanti: he it was,
Found entertaining unawares—if not
An angel, yet a youth in search of one.

Why this revealment after reticence?
Wherefore, beginning "Millefleurs," end at all
Steiner, Muhlhausen, and the ugly rest?
Because the unsocial purse-controlling wight,
Carlino Centofanti, made aware
By misadventure that his bounty, crumbs
From table, comforted a visitant,
Took churlish leave, and left, too, debts to pay.
Loaded with debts, the lady needs must bring
Her soul to bear assistance from a friend
Beside that paltry ring, three Louis'-worth;
And therefore might the little circumstance
That Monsieur Léonce had the rummaging
Of old Papa's shop in the Place Vendôme,
Pass, perhaps, not so unobservably.

Frail shadow of a woman in the flesh,
These very eyes of mine saw yesterday,
Would I re-tell this story of your woes,
Would I have heart to do you detriment
By pinning all this shame and sorrow plain
To that poor chignon,—staying with me still,
Though form and face have well-nigh faded now,—
But that men read it, rough in brutal print,
As two years since some functionary's voice
Rattled all this—and more by very much—
Into the ear of vulgar Court and crowd?
Whence, by reverberation, rumblings grew
To what had proved a week-long roar in France
Had not the dreadful cannonry drowned all.
Was, now, the answer of your advocate
More than just this? "The shame fell long ago,
The sorrow keeps increasing: God forbid
We judge man by the faults of youth in age!"
Permit me the expression of a hope
Your youth proceeded like your avenue,
Stepping by bush, and tree, and taller tree,
Until, columnar, at the house they end.

So might your creeping youth columnar rise
And reach, by year and year, symmetrical,
To where all shade stops short, shade's service done.
Bushes on either side, and boughs above,
Darken, deform the path else sun would streak;
And, cornered halfway somewhere, I suspect
Stagnation and a horse-pond: hurry past!
For here 's the house, the happy half-and-half
Existence—such as stands for happiness
True and entire, howe'er the squeamish talk!
Twenty years long, you may have loved this man;
He must have loved you; that 's a pleasant life,
Whatever was your right to lead the same.
The white domestic pigeon pairs secure,
Nay, does mere duty by bestowing egg
In authorized compartment, warm and safe,
Boarding about, and gilded spire above,
Hoisted on pole, to dogs' and eats' despair!
But I have spied a veriest trap of twigs
On tree-top, every straw a thievery,
Where the wild dove—despite the fowler's snare,
The sportsman's shot, the urchin's stone—crooned gay,
And solely gave her heart to what she hatched,
Nor minded a malignant world below.
I throw first stone forsooth? 'T is mere assault
Of playful sugarplum against your cheek,
Which, if it makes cheek tingle, wipes off rouge!
You, my worst woman? Ah, that touches pride,
Puts on his mettle the exhibitor
Of Night-caps, if you taunt him "This, no doubt,—
Now we have got to Female-garniture,—
Crowns your collection, Reddest of the row!"
O unimaginative ignorance
Of what dye's depth keeps best apart from worst
In womankind!—how heaven's own pure may seem
To blush aurorally beside such blanched
Divineness as the women-wreaths named White:
While hell, eruptive and fuliginous,
Sickens to very pallor as I point
Her place to a Red clout called woman too!
Hail, heads that ever had such glory once
Touch you a moment, like God's cloven tongues
Of fire! your lambent aureoles lost may leave
You marked yet, dear beyond true diadems!
And hold, each foot, nor spurn, to man's disgrace,
What other twist of fetid rag may fall!
Let slink into the sewer the cupping-cloth!

Lucie, much solaced, I re-finger you,
The medium article; if ruddy-marked
With iron-mould, your cambric,—clean at least
From poison-speck of rot and purulence!
Lucie Muhlhausen said—"Such thing am I:
Love me, or love me not!" Miranda said,
"I do love, more than ever, most for this."
The revelation of the very truth
Proved the concluding necessary shake
Which bids the tardy mixture crystallize
Or else stay ever liquid: shoot up shaft,
Durably diamond, or evaporate—
Sluggish solution through a minute's slip.
Monsieur Léonce Miranda took his soul
In both his hands, as if it were a vase,
To see what came of the convulsion there,
And found, amid subsidence, love new-born
So sparklingly resplendent, old was new.
"Whatever be my lady's present, past,
Or future, this is certain of my soul,
I love her! in despite of all I know,
Defiance of the much I have to fear,
I venture happiness on what I hope,
And love her from this day forevermore!
No prejudice to old profound respect
For certain Powers! I trust they bear in mind
A most peculiar case, and straighten out
What 's crooked there, before we close accounts.
Renounce the world for them—some day I will:
Meantime, to me let her become the world!"

Thus, mutely might our friend soliloquize
Over the tradesmen's bills, his Clara's gift—
In the apartment, Coliseum Street,
Carlino Centofanti's legacy,
Provided rent and taxes were discharged—
In face of Steiner now, De Millefleurs once,
The tailor's wife and runaway confessed.

On such a lady if election light,
(According to a social prejudice,)
If henceforth "all the world" she constitute
For any lover,—needs must he renounce
Our world in ordinary, walked about
By couples loving as its laws prescribe,—
Renunciation sometimes difficult.
But, in this instance, time and place and thing
Combined to simplify experiment,

And make Miranda, in the current phrase,
Master the situation passably.

For first facility, his brother died—
Who was, I should have told you, confidant,
Adviser, referee, and substitute,
All from a distance: but I knew how soon
This younger brother, lost in Portugal,
Had to depart and leave our friend at large.
Cut off abruptly from companionship
With brother-soul of bulk about as big,
(Obvious recipient—by intelligence
And sympathy, poor little pair of souls—
Of much affection and some foolishness,)
Monsieur Léonce Miranda, meant to lean
By nature, needs must shift the leaning-place
To his love's bosom from his brother's neck,
Or fall flat unrelieved of freight sublime.

Next died the lord of the Aladdin's cave,
Master o' the mint, and keeper of the keys
Of chests chokefull with gold and silver changed
By Art to forms where wealth forgot itself,
And caskets where reposed each pullet-egg
Of diamond, slipping flame from fifty slants.
In short, the father of the family
Took his departure also from our scene,
Leaving a fat succession to his heir
Monsieur Léonce Miranda,—"fortunate,
If ever man was, in a father's death,"
(So commented the world,—not he, too kind,
Could that be, rather than scarce kind enough)
Indisputably fortunate so far,
That little of incumbrance in his path,
Which money kicks aside, would lie there long.

And finally, a rough but wholesome shock,
An accident which comes to kill or cure,
A jerk which mends a dislocated joint!
Such happy chance, at cost of twinge, no doubt,
Into the socket back again put truth,
And stopped the limb from longer dragging lie.
For love suggested, "Better shamble on,
And bear your lameness with what grace you may!"
And but for this rude wholesome accident,
Continuance of disguise and subterfuge,
Retention of first falsehood as to name
And nature in the lady, might have proved

Too necessary for abandonment.
Monsieur Léonce Miranda probably
Had else been loath to cast the mask aside,
So politic, so self-preservative,
Therefore so pardonable—though so wrong!
For see the bugbear in the background! Breathe
But ugly name, and wind is sure to waft
The husband news of the wife's whereabout:
From where he lies perdue in London town,
Forth steps the needy tailor on the stage,
Deity-like from dusk machine of fog,
And claims his consort, or his consort's worth
In rubies which her price is far above.
Hard to propitiate, harder to oppose,—
Who but the man's self came to banish fear,
A pleasant apparition, such as shocks
A moment, tells a tale, then goes for good!

Monsieur Ulysse Muhlhausen proved no less
Nor more than "Gustave," lodging opposite
Monsieur Léonce Miranda's diamond-cave
And ruby-mine, and lacking little thence
Save that its gnome would keep the captive safe,
Never return his Clara to his arms.
For why? He was become the man in vogue,
The indispensable to who went clothed
Nor cared encounter Paris fashion's blame,—
Such miracle could London absence work.
Rolling in riches—so translate "the vogue"—
Rather his object was to keep off claw
Should griffin scent the gold, should wife lay claim
To lawful portion at a future day,
Than tempt his partner from her private spoils.
Best forage each for each, nor coupled hunt!

Pursuantly, one morning,—knock at door
With knuckle, dry authoritative cough,
And easy stamp of foot, broke startlingly
On household slumber, Coliseum Street:
"Admittance in the name of Law!" In marched
The Commissary and subordinate.
One glance sufficed them. "A marital pair:
We certify, and bid good morning, sir!
Madame, a thousand pardons!" Whereupon
Monsieur Ulysse Muhlhausen, otherwise
Called "Gustave" for conveniency of trade,
Deposing in due form complaint of wrong,
Made his demand of remedy—divorce

From bed, board, share of name, and part in goods.
Monsieur Léonce Miranda owned his fault,
Protested his pure ignorance, from first
To last, of rights infringed in "Gustave's" case:
Submitted him to judgment. Law decreed
"Body and goods be henceforth separate!"
And thereupon each party took its way,
This right, this left, rejoicing, to abide
Estranged yet amicable, opposites
In life as in respective dwelling-place.
Still does one read on his establishment
Huge-lettered "Gustave,"—gold out-glittering
"Miranda, goldsmith," just across the street—
"A first-rate hand at riding-habits"—say
The instructed—"special cut of chamber-robes."

Thus by a rude in seeming—rightlier judged
Beneficent surprise, publicity
Stopped further fear and trembling, and what tale
Cowardice thinks a covert: one bold splash
Into the mid-shame, and the shiver ends,
Though cramp and drowning may begin perhaps.

To cite just one more point which crowned success:
Madame, Miranda's mother, most of all
An obstacle to his projected life
In license, as a daughter of the Church,
Duteous, exemplary, severe by right—
Moreover one most thoroughly beloved
Without a rival till the other sort
Possessed her son,—first storm of anger spent,
She seemed, though grumblingly and grudgingly,
To let be what needs must be, acquiesce.
"With heaven—accommodation possible!"
Saint Sganarelle had preached with such effect,
She saw now mitigating circumstance.
"The erring one was most unfortunate,
No question: but worse Magdalens repent.
Were Clara free, did only Law allow,
What fitter choice in marriage could have made
Léonce or anybody?" 'T is alleged
And evidenced, I find, by advocate,
"Never did she consider such a tie
As baleful, springe to snap whate'er the cost."
And when the couple were in safety once
At Clairvaux, motherly, considerate,
She shrank not from advice. "Since safe you be,
Safely abide! for winter, I know well,

Is troublesome in a cold country-house.
I recommend the south room that we styled,
Your sire and I, the winter-chamber."

Chance
Or purpose,—who can read the mystery?—
Combined, I say, to bid "Intrench yourself,
Monsieur Léonce Miranda, on this turf,
About this flower, so firmly that, as tent
Rises on every side around you both,
The question shall become,—Which arrogates
Stability, this tent or those far towers?
May not the temporary structure suit
The stable circuit, co-exist in peace?—
Always until the proper time, no fear!
'Lay flat your tent!' is easier said than done."

So, with the best of auspices, betook
Themselves Léonce Miranda and his bride—
Provisionary—to their Clairvaux house,
Never to leave it—till the proper time.

I told you what was Clairvaux-Priory
Ere the improper time: an old demesne
With memories,—relic half, and ruin whole,—
The very place, then, to repair the wits
Worn out with Paris-traffic, when its lord,
Miranda's father, took his month of ease
Purchased by industry. What contrast here!
Repose, and solitude, and healthy ways!
That ticking at the back of head, he took
For motion of an inmate, stopped at once,
Proved nothing but the pavement's rattle left
Behind at Paris: here was holiday!
Welcome the quaint succeeding to the spruce,
The large and lumbersome and—might he breathe
In whisper to his own ear—dignified
And gentry-fashioned old-style haunts of sleep!
Palatial gloomy chambers for parade,
And passage-lengths of lost significance,
Never constructed as receptacle,
At his odd hours, for him their actual lord
By dint of diamond-dealing, goldsmithry.
Therefore Miranda's father chopped and changed
Nor roof-tile nor yet floor-brick, undismayed
By rains a-top or rats at bottom there.
Such contrast is so piquant for a month!
But now arrived quite other occupants

Whose cry was "Permanency,—life and death
Here, here, not elsewhere, change is all we dread!"
Their dwelling-place must be adapted, then,
To inmates, no mere truants from the town,
No temporary sojourners, forsooth,
At Clairvaux: change it into Paradise!

Fair friend,—who listen and let talk, alas!—
You would, in even such a state of things,
Pronounce,—or am I wrong?—for bidding stay
The old-world inconvenience, fresh as found.
All folk of individuality
Prefer to be reminded, now and then,
Though at the cost of vulgar cosiness,
That the shell-outside only harbors man
The vital and progressive, meant to build,
When build he may, with quite a difference,
Some time, in that far land we dream about,
Where every man is his own architect.
But then the couple here in question, each
At one in project for a happy life,
Were by no acceptation of the word
So individual that they must aspire
To architecture all-appropriate,
And, therefore, in this world impossible:
They needed house to suit the circumstance,
Proprietors, not tenants for a term.
Despite a certain marking, here and there,
Of fleecy black or white distinguishment,
These vulgar sheep wore the flock's uniform.
They love the country, they renounce the town?
They gave a kick, as our Italians say,
To Paris ere it turned and kicked themselves!
Acquaintances might prove too hard to seek,
Or the reverse of hard to find, perchance,
Since Monsieur Gustave's apparition there.
And let me call remark upon the list
Of notabilities invoked, in Court
At Vire, to witness, by their phrases culled
From correspondence, what was the esteem
Of those we pay respect to, for "the pair
Whereof they knew the inner life," 't is said.
Three, and three only, answered the appeal.
First Monsieur Vaillant, music-publisher,
"Begs Madame will accept civilities."
Next Alexandre Dumas,—sire, not son,—
"Sends compliments to Madame and to you."
And last—but now prepare for England's voice!

I will not mar nor make—here 's word for word—
"A rich proprietor of Paris, he
To whom belonged that beauteous Bagatelle
Close to the wood of Boulogne, Hertford hight,
Assures of homages and compliments
Affectionate"—not now Miranda but
"Madame Muhlhausen." (Was this friend, the Duke
Redoubtable in rivalry before?)
Such was the evidence when evidence
Was wanted, then if ever, to the worth
Whereat acquaintances in Paris prized
Monsieur Léonce Miranda's household charm.
No wonder, then, his impulse was to live,
In Norman solitude, the Paris life:
Surround himself with Art transported thence,
And nature like those famed Elysian Fields:
Then, warm up the right color out of both,
By Boulevard friendships tempted to come taste
How Paris lived again in little there.

Monsieur Léonce Miranda practised Art.
Do let a man for once live as man likes!
Politics? Spend your life, to spare the world's:
Improve each unit by some particle
Of joy the more, deteriorate the orb
Entire, your own: poor profit, dismal loss!
Write books, paint pictures, or make music—since
Your nature leans to such life-exercise!
Ay, but such exercise begins too soon,
Concludes too late, demands life whole and sole,
Artistry being battle with the age
It lives in! Half life,—silence, while you learn
What has been done; the other half,—attempt
At speech, amid world's wail of wonderment—
"Here 's something done was never done before!"
To be the very breath that moves the age
Means not to have breath drive you bubble-like
Before it—but yourself to blow: that 's strain;
Strain's worry through the lifetime, till there 's peace;
We know where peace expects the artist-soul.

Monsieur Léonce Miranda knew as much.
Therefore in Art he nowise cared to be
Creative; but creation, that had birth
In storminess long years before was born
Monsieur Léonce Miranda,—Art, enjoyed
Like fleshly objects of the chase that tempt
In auxiliary, not in rapture these might feast

The dilettante, furnish tavern-fare
Open to all with purses open too.
To sit free and take tribute seigneur-like—
Now, not too lavish of acknowledgment,
Now, self-indulgently profuse of pay.
Always Art's seigneur, not Art's serving-man,
Whate'er the style and title and degree,—
That is the quiet life and easy death
Monsieur Léonce Miranda would approve
Wholly—provided (back I go again
To the first simile) that while glasses clink,
And viands steam, and banqueting laughs high,
All that 's outside the temporary tent,
The dim grim outline of the circuit-wall,
Forgets to menace "Soon or late will drop
Pavilion, soon or late you needs must march,
And laggards will be sorry they were slack!
Always—unless excuse sound plausible!"

Monsieur Léonce Miranda knew as much:
Whence his determination just to paint
So creditably as might help the eye
To comprehend how painter's eye grew dim
Ere it produced L'Ingegno's piece of work—
So to become musician that his ear
Should judge, by its own tickling and turmoil,
Who made the Solemn Mass might well die deaf—
So cultivate a literary knack
That, by experience how it wiles the time,
He might imagine how a poet, rapt
In rhyming wholly, grew so poor at last
By carelessness about his banker's-book,
That the Sieur Boileau (to provoke our smile)
Began abruptly,—when he paid devoir
To Louis Quatorze as he dined in state,—
"Sire, send a drop of broth to Pierre Corneille
Now dying and in want of sustenance!"
—I say, these half-hour playings at life's toil,
Diversified by billiards, riding, sport—
With now and then a visitor—Dumas,
Hertford—to check no aspiration's flight—
While Clara, like a diamond in the dark,
Should extract shining from what else were shade,
And multiply chance rays a million-fold,—
How could he doubt that all offence outside,—
Wrong to the towers, which, pillowed on the turf,
He thus shut eyes to,—were as good as gone?

So, down went Clairvaux-Priory to dust,
And up there rose, in lieu, yon structure gay
Above the Norman ghosts: and where the stretch
Of barren country girdled house about,
Behold the Park, the English preference!
Thus made undoubtedly a desert smile
Monsieur Léonce Miranda.

Ay, but she?
One should not so merge soul in soul, you think?
And I think: only, let us wait, nor want
Two things at once—her turn will come in time.
A cork-float danced upon the tide, we saw,
This morning, blinding-bright with briny dews:
There was no disengaging soaked from sound,
Earth-product from the sister-element.
But when we turn, the tide will turn, I think,
And bare on beach will lie exposed the buoy:
A very proper time to try, with foot
And even finger, which was buoying wave,
Which merely buoyant substance,—power to lift,
And power to be sent skyward passively.
Meanwhile, no separation of the pair!

III

And so slipt pleasantly away five years
Of Paradisiac dream; till, as there flit
Premonitory symptoms, pricks of pain,
Because the dreamer has to start awake
And find disease dwelt active all the while
In head or stomach through his night-long sleep,—
So happened here disturbance to content.

Monsieur Léonce Miranda's last of cares,
Ere he composed himself, had been to make
Provision that, while sleeping safe he lay,
Somebody else should, dragon-like, let fall
Never a lid, coiled round the apple-stem,
But watch the precious fruitage. Somebody
Kept shop, in short, played Paris substitute.
Himself, shrewd, well-trained, early-exercised,
Could take in, at an eye-glance, luck or loss—
Know commerce throve, though lazily uplift
On elbow merely: leave his bed forsooth?
Such active service was the substitute's.

But one October morning, at first drop
Of appled gold, first summons to be grave
Because rough Autumn's play turns earnest now,
Monsieur Léonce Miranda was required
In Paris to take counsel, face to face,
With Madame-mother: and be rated, too,
Roundly at certain items of expense
Whereat the government provisional,
The Paris substitute and shopkeeper,
Shook head, and talked of funds inadequate:
Oh, in the long run,—not if remedy
Occurred betimes! Else,—tap the generous bole
Too near the quick,—it withers to the root—
Leafy, prolific, golden apple-tree,
"Miranda," sturdy in the Place Vendôme!

"What is this reckless life you lead?" began
Her greeting she whom most he feared and loved,
Madame Miranda. "Luxury, extravagance
Sardanapalus' self might emulate,—
Did your good father's money go for this?
Where are the fruits of education, where
The morals which at first distinguished you,
The faith which promised to adorn your age?
And why such wastefulness outbreaking now,
When heretofore you loved economy?
Explain this pulling-down and building-up
Poor Clairvaux, which your father bought because
Clairvaux he found it, and so left to you,
Not a gilt-gingerbread big baby-house!
True, we could somehow shake head and shut eye
To what was past prevention on our part—
This reprehensible illicit bond:
We, in a manner, winking, watched consort
Our modest well-conducted pious son
With Delilah: we thought the smoking flax
Would smoulder soon away and end in snuff!
Is spark to strengthen, prove consuming fire?
No lawful family calls Clairvaux 'home'—
Why play that fool of Scripture whom the voice
Admonished 'Whose to-night shall be those things
Provided for thy morning jollity?'
To take one specimen of pure caprice
Out of the heap conspicuous in the plan,—
Puzzle of change, I call it,—titled big
'Clairvaux Restored:' what means this Belvedere?
This Tower, stuck like a fool's-cap on the roof—
Do you intend to soar to heaven from thence?

Tower, truly! Better had you planted turf—
More fitly would you dig yourself a hole
Beneath it for the final journey's help!
O we poor parents—could we prophesy!"
Léonce was found affectionate enough
To man, to woman, child, bird, beast, alike;
But all affection, all one fire of heart
Flaming toward Madame-mother. Had she posed
The question plainly at the outset "Choose!
Cut clean in half your all-the-world of love,
The mother and the mistress: then resolve,
Take me or take her, throw away the one!"—
He might have made the choice and marred my tale.
But, much I apprehend, the problem put
Was, "Keep both halves, yet do no detriment
To either! Prize each opposite in turn!"
Hence, while he prized at worth the Clairvaux-life
With all its tolerated naughtiness,
He, visiting in fancy Quai Rousseau,
Saw, cornered in the cosiest nook of all,
That range of rooms through number Thirty-three,
The lady-mother bent o'er her Bézique
While Monsieur Curé This, and Sister That,—
Superior of no matter what good House—
Did duty for Duke Hertford and Dumas,
Nay—at his mother's age—for Clara's self.
At Quai Rousseau, things comfortable thus,
Why should poor Clairvaux prove so troublesome?
She played at cards, he built a Belvedere.
But here 's the difference: she had reached the Towers
And there took pastime: he was still on Turf—
Though fully minded that, when once he marched,
No sportive fancy should distract him more.

In brief, the man was angry with himself,
With her, with all the world and much beside:
And so the unseemly words were interchanged
Which crystallize what else evaporates,
And make mere misty petulance grow hard
And sharp inside each softness, heart and soul.
Monsieur Léonce Miranda flung at last
Out of doors, fever-flushed: and there the Seine
Rolled at his feet, obsequious remedy
For fever, in a cold autumnal flow.
"Go and be rid of memory in a bath!"
Craftily whispered Who besets the ear
On such occasions.

Done as soon as dreamed.
Back shivers poor Léonce to bed—where else?
And there he lies a month 'twixt life and death,
Raving. "Remorse of conscience!" friends opine.
"Sirs, it may partly prove so," represents
Beaumont—(the family physician, he
Whom last year's Commune murdered, do you mind?)
Beaumont reports, "There is some active cause,
More than mere pungency of quarrel past,—
Cause that keeps adding other food to fire.
I hear the words and know the signs, I say!
Dear Madame, you have read the Book of Saints,
How Antony was tempted? As for me,
Poor heathen, 't is by pictures I am taught.
I say then, I see standing here,—between
Me and my patient, and that crucifix
You very properly would interpose—
A certain woman-shape, one white appeal,
'Will you leave me, then, me, me, me for her?'
Since cold Seine could not quench this flame, since flare
Of fever does not redden it away,—
Be rational, indulgent, mute—should chance
Come to the rescue—Providence, I mean—
The while I blister and phlebotomize!"

Well, somehow rescued by whatever power,
At month's end, back again conveyed himself
Monsieur Léonce Miranda, worn to rags,
Nay, tinder: stuff irreparably spoiled,
Though kindly hand should stitch and patch its best.
Clairvaux in Autumn is restorative.
A friend stitched on, patched ever. All the same,
Clairvaux looked grayer than a month ago.
Unglossed was shrubbery, unglorified
Each copse, so wealthy once; the garden-plots.
The orchard-walks, showed dearth and dreariness.
The sea lay out at distance crammed by cloud
Into a leaden wedge; and sorrowful
Sulked field and pasture with persistent rain.
Nobody came so far from Paris now:
Friends did their duty by an invalid
Whose convalescence claimed entire repose.
Only a single ministrant was stanch
At quiet reparation of the stuff—
Monsieur Léonce Miranda, worn to rags:
But she was Clara and the world beside.

Another month, the year packed up his plagues

And sullenly departed, peddler-like,
As apprehensive old-world ware might show
To disadvantage when the newcomer,
Merchant of novelties, young 'Sixty-eight,
With brand-new bargains, whistled o'er the lea.
Things brightened somewhat o'er the Christmas hearth,
As Clara plied assiduously her task.

"Words are but words and wind. Why let the wind
Sing in your ear, bite, sounding, to your brain?
Old folk and young folk, still at odds, of course!
Age quarrels because Spring puts forth a leaf
While Winter has a mind that boughs stay bare;
Or rather—worse than quarrel—age descries
Propriety in preaching life to death.
'Enjoy nor youth, nor Clairvaux, nor poor me?'
Dear Madame, you enjoy your age, 't is thought!
Your number Thirty-three on Quai Rousseau
Cost fifty times the price of Clairvaux, tipped
Even with our prodigious Belvedere;
You entertain the Curé,—we, Dumas:
We play charades, while you prefer Bézique:
Do lead your own life and let ours alone!
Cross Old Year shall have done his worst, my friend!
Here comes gay New Year with a gift, no doubt!
Look up and let in light that longs to shine—
One flash of light, and where will darkness hide?
Your cold makes me too cold, love! Keep me warm!"

Whereat Léonce Miranda raised his head
From his two white thin hands, and forced a smile,
And spoke: "I do look up, and see your light
Above me! Let New Year contribute warmth—
I shall refuse no fuel that may blaze."
Nor did he. Three days after, just a spark
From Paris, answered by a snap at Caen
Or whither reached the telegraphic wire:
"Quickly to Paris! On arrival, learn
Why you are wanted!" Curt and critical!

Off starts Léonce, one fear from head to foot;
Caen, Rouen, Paris, as the railway helps;
Then come the Quai and Number Thirty-three.
"What is the matter, concierge?"—a grimace!
He mounts the staircase, makes for the main seat
Of dreadful mystery which draws him there—
Bursts in upon a bedroom known too well—
There lies all left now of the mother once

Tapers define the stretch of rigid white,
Nor want there ghastly velvets of the grave.
A blackness sits on either side at watch,
Sisters, good souls but frightful all the same,
Silent: a priest is spokesman for his corpse.
"Dead, through Léonce Miranda! stricken down
Without a minute's warning, yesterday!
What did she say to you, and you to her,
Two months ago? This is the consequence!
The doctors have their name for the disease;
I, you, and God say—heart-break, nothing more!"
Monsieur Léonce Miranda, like a stone
Fell at the bedfoot and found respite so,
While the priest went to tell the company.
What follows you are free to disbelieve.
It may be true or false that this good priest
Had taken his instructions,—who shall blame?—
From quite another quarter than, perchance,
Monsieur Léonce Miranda might suppose
Would offer solace in such pressing need.
All he remembered of his kith and kin
Was, they were worthily his substitutes
In commerce, did their work and drew their pay.
But they remembered, in addition, this—
They fairly might expect inheritance,
As nearest kin, called Family by law
And gospel both. Now, since Miranda's life
Showed nothing like abatement of distaste
For conjugality, but preference
Continued and confirmed of that smooth chain
Which slips and leaves no knot behind, no heir—
Presumption was, the man, become mature,
Would at a calculable day discard
His old and outworn ... what we blush to name,
And make society the just amends;
Scarce by a new attachment—Heaven forbid!
Still less by lawful marriage: that 's reserved
For those who make a proper choice at first—
Not try both courses and would grasp in age
The very treasure, youth preferred to spurn!
No! putting decently such thought aside,
The penitent must rather give his powers
To such a reparation of the past
As, edifying kindred, makes them rich.
Now, how would it enrich prospectively
The Cousins, if he lavished such expense
On Clairvaux?—pretty as a toy, but then
As toy, so much productive and no more!

If all the outcome of the goldsmith's shop
Went to gild Clairvaux, where remain the funds
For Cousinry to spread out lap and take?
This must be thought of and provided for.
I give it you a mere conjecture, mind!
To help explain the wholesome unannounced
Intelligence, the shock that startled guilt,
The scenic show, much yellow, black and white
By taper-shine, the nuns—portentous pair,
And, more than all, the priest's admonishment—
"No flattery of self! You murdered her!
The gray lips, silent now, reprove by mine.
You wasted all your living, rioted
In harlotry—she warned and I repeat!
No warning had she, for she needed none:
If this should be the last yourself receive?"
Done for the best, no doubt, though clumsily,—
Such, and so startling, the reception here.
You hardly wonder if down fell at once
The tawdry tent, pictorial, musical,
Poetical, besprent with hearts and darts;
Its cobweb-work, betinselled stitchery,
Lay dust about our sleeper on the turf,
And showed the outer towers distinct and dread.

Senseless he fell, and long he lay, and much
Seemed salutary in his punishment
To planners and performers of the piece.
When pain ends, pardon prompt may operate.
There was a good attendance close at hand,
Waiting the issue in the great saloon,
Cousins with consolation and advice.

All things thus happily performed to point,
No wonder at success commensurate.
Once swooning stopped, once anguish subsequent
Raved out,—a sudden resolution chilled
His blood and changed his swimming eyes to stone,
As the poor fellow raised himself upright,
Collected strength, looked, once for all, his look,
Then, turning, put officious help aside
And passed from out the chamber. "For affairs!"
So he announced himself to the saloon:
"We owe a duty to the living too!"—
Monsieur Léonce Miranda tried to smile.
How did the hearts of Cousinry rejoice
At their stray sheep returning thus to fold,
As, with a dignity, precision, sense,

All unsuspected in the man before,
Monsieur Léonce Miranda made minute
Detail of his intended scheme of life
Thenceforward and forever. "Vanity
Was ended: its redemption must begin—
And, certain, would continue; but since life
Was awfully uncertain—witness here!—
Behooved him lose no moment but discharge
Immediate burden of the world's affairs
On backs that kindly volunteered to crouch.
Cousins, with easier conscience, blamelessly
Might carry on the goldsmith's trade, in brief,
Uninterfered with by its lord who late
Was used to supervise and take due tithe.
A stipend now sufficed his natural need:
Themselves should fix what sum allows man live.
But half a dozen words concisely plain
Might, first of all, make sure that, on demise,
Monsieur Léonce Miranda's property
Passed by bequeathment, every particle,
To the right heirs, the cousins of his heart.
As for that woman—they would understand!
This was a step must take her by surprise!
It were too cruel did he snatch away
Decent subsistence. She was young, and fair,
And ... and attractive! Means must be supplied
To save her from herself, and from the world,
And ... from anxieties might haunt him else
When he were fain have other thoughts in mind."

It was a sight to melt a stone, that thaw
Of rigid disapproval into dew
Of sympathy, as each extended palm
Of cousin hasted to enclose those five
Cold fingers, tendered so mistrustfully,
Despairingly of condonation now!
You would have thought,—at every fervent shake,
In reassurance of those timid tips,—
The penitent had squeezed, considerate,
By way of fee into physician's hand
For physicking his soul, some diamond knob.

And now let pass a week. Once more behold
The same assemblage in the same saloon,
Waiting the entry of protagonist
Monsieur Léonce Miranda. "Just a week
Since the death-day,—was ever man transformed
Like this man?" questioned cousin of his mate.

Last seal to the repentance had been set
Three days before, at Sceaux in neighborhood
Of Paris where they laid with funeral pomp
Mother by father. Let me spare the rest:
How the poor fellow, in his misery,
Buried hot face and bosom, where heaped snow
Offered assistance, at the grave's black edge,
And there lay, till uprooted by main force
From where he prayed to grow and ne'er again
Walk earth unworthily as heretofore.
It is not with impunity priests teach
The doctrine he was dosed with from his youth—
"Pain to the body—profit to the soul;
Corporeal pleasure—so much woe to pay
When disembodied spirit gives account."

However, woe had done its worst, this time.
Three days allow subsidence of much grief.
Already, regular and equable,
Forward went purpose to effect. At once
The testament was written, signed and sealed.
Disposer of the commerce—that took time,
And would not suffer by a week's delay;
But the immediate, the imperious need,
The call demanding of the Cousinry
Co-operation, what convened them thus,
Was—how and when should deputation march
To Coliseum Street, the old abode
Of wickedness, and there acquaint—oh, shame!
Her, its old inmate, who had followed up
And lay in wait in the old haunt for prey—
That they had rescued, they possessed Léonce,
Whose loathing at recapture equalled theirs—
Upbraid that sinner with her sinfulness,
Impart the fellow-sinner's firm resolve
Never to set eyes on her face again:
Then, after stipulations strict but just,
Hand her the first instalment—moderate
Enough, no question—of her salary:
Admonish for the future, and so end.—
All which good purposes, decided on
Sufficiently, were waiting full effect
When presently the culprit should appear.

Somehow appearance was delayed too long;
Chatting and chirping sunk inconsciously
To silence, nay, unassiness, at length

Alarm, till—anything for certitude!—
A peeper was commissioned to explore,
At keyhole, what the laggard's task might be—
What caused so palpable a disrespect!

Back came the tiptoe cousin from his quest.
"Monsieur Léonce was busy," he believed,
"Contemplating—those love-letters, perhaps,
He always carried, as if precious stones,
About with him. He read, one after one,
Some sort of letters. But his back was turned.
The empty coffer open at his side,
He leant on elbow by the mantelpiece
Before the hearth-fire; big and blazing too."

"Better he shovelled them all in at once,
And burned the rubbish!" was a cousin's quip,
Warming his own hands at the fire the while,
I told you, snow had fallen outside, I think.

When suddenly a cry, a host of cries,
Screams, hubbub and confusion thrilled the room.
All by a common impulse rushed thence, reached
The late death-chamber, tricked with trappings still,
Skulls, crossbones, and such moral broidery.
Madame Muhlhausen might have played the witch,
Dropped down the chimney and appalled Léonce
By some proposal, "Parting touch of hand!"
If she but touched his foolish hand, you know!

Something had happened quite contrariwise.
Monsieur Léonce Miranda, one by one,
Had read the letters and the love they held,
And, that task finished, had required his soul
To answer frankly what the prospect seemed
Of his own love's departure—pledged to part!
Then, answer being unmistakable,
He had replaced the letters quietly,
Shut coffer, and so, grasping either side
By its convenient handle, plunged the whole—
Letters and coffer and both hands to boot—
Into the burning grate and held them there.
"Burn, burn, and purify my past!" said he,
Calmly, as if he felt no pain at all.

In vain they pulled him from the torture-place:
The strong man, with the soul of tenfold strength,
Broke from their clutch: and there again smiled he,

The miserable hands re-bathed in fire—
Constant to that ejaculation, "Burn,
Burn, purify!" And when, combining force.
They fairly dragged the victim out of reach
Of further harm, he had no hands to hurt—
Two horrible remains of right and left,
"Whereof the bones, phalanges formerly,
Carbonized, were still crackling with the flame,"
Said Beaumont. And he fought them all the while:
"Why am I hindered when I would be pure?
Why leave the sacrifice still incomplete?
She holds me, I must have more hands to burn!"
They were the stronger, though, and bound him fast.

Beaumont was in attendance presently.
"What did I tell you? Preachment to the deaf!
I wish he had been deafer when they preached,
Those priests! But wait till next Republic comes!"

As for Léonce, a single sentiment
Possessed his soul and occupied his tongue—
Absolute satisfaction at the deed.
Never he varied, 't is observable,
Nor in the stage of agonies (which proved
Absent without leave,—science seemed to think),
Nor yet in those three months' febricity
Which followed,—never did he vary tale—
Remaining happy beyond utterance.
"Ineffable beatitude"—I quote
The words, I cannot give the smile—"such bliss
Abolished pain! Pain might or might not be:
He felt in heaven, where flesh desists to fret.
Purified now and henceforth, all the past
Reduced to ashes with the flesh defiled!
Why all those anxious faces round his bed?
What was to pity in their patient, pray,
When doctor came and went, and Cousins watched?
—Kindness, but in pure waste!" he said and smiled.
And if a trouble would at times disturb
The ambrosial mood, it came from other source
Than the corporeal transitory pang.
"If sacrifice be incomplete!" cried he—
"If ashes have not sunk reduced to dust,
To nullity! If atoms coalesce
Till something grow, grow, get to be a shape
I hate, I hoped to burn away from me!
She is my body, she and I are one,
Yet, all the same, there, there at bedfoot stands

The woman wound about my flesh and blood,
There, the arms open, the more wonderful,
The whiter for the burning ... Vanish thou!
Avaunt, fiend's self found in the form I wore!"

"Whereat," said Beaumont, "since his hands were gone,
The patient in a frenzy kicked and kicked
To keep off some imagined visitant.
So will it prove as long as priests may preach
Spiritual terrors!" groaned the evidence
Of Beaumont that his patient was stark mad—
Produced in time and place: of which anon.
"Mad, or why thus insensible to pain?
Body and soul are one thing, with two names
For more or less elaborated stuff."

Such is the new Religio Medici.
Though antiquated faith held otherwise,
Explained that body is not soul, but just
Soul's servant: that, if soul be satisfied,
Possess already joy or pain enough,
It uses to ignore, as master may,
What increase, joy or pain, its servant brings—
Superfluous contribution: soul, once served,
Has naught to do with body's service more.
Each, speculated on exclusively,
As if its office were the only one,
Body or soul, either shows service paid
In joy and pain, that 's blind and objectless—
A servant's toiling for no master's good—
Or else shows good received and put to use,
As if within soul's self grew joy and pain,
Nor needed body for a ministrant.
I note these old unscientific ways:
Poor Beaumont cannot: for the Commune ruled
Next year, and ere they shot his priests, shot him.

Monsieur Léonce Miranda raved himself
To rest; lay three long months in bliss or bale,
Inactive, anyhow: more need that heirs,
His natural protectors, should assume
The management, bestir their cousinship,
And carry out that purpose of reform
Such tragic work now made imperative.
A deputation, with austerity,
Nay, sternness, bore her sentence to the fiend
Aforesaid,—she at watch for turn of wheel
And fortune's favor, Street—you know the name.

A certain roughness seemed appropriate: "You—
Steiner, Muhlhausen, whatsoe'er your name,
Cause whole and sole of this catastrophe!"—
And so forth, introduced the embassage.

"Monsieur Léonce Miranda was divorced
Once and forever from his—ugly word.
Himself had gone for good to Portugal;
They came empowered to act and stipulate.
Hold! no discussion! Terms were settled now:
So much of present and prospective pay,
But also—good engagement in plain terms
She never seek renewal of the past!"

This little harmless tale produced effect.
Madame Muhlhausen owned her sentence just,
Its execution gentle. "Stern their phrase,
These kinsfolk with a right she recognized—
But kind its import probably, which now
Her agitation, her bewilderment,
Rendered too hard to understand, perhaps.
Let them accord the natural delay,
And she would ponder and decide. Meantime,
So far was she from wish to follow friend
Who fled her, that she would not budge from place—
Now that her friend was fled to Portugal,—
Never! She leave this Coliseum Street?
No, not a footstep!" she assured them.

So—
They saw they might have left that tale untold
When, after some weeks more were gone to waste,
Recovery seemed incontestable,
And the poor mutilated figure, once
The gay and glancing fortunate young spark,
Miranda, humble and obedient took
The doctor's counsel, issued sad and slow
From precincts of the sick-room, tottered down,
And out, and into carriage for fresh air,
And so drove straight to Coliseum Street,
And tottered upstairs, knocked, and in a trice
Was clasped in the embrace of whom you know—
With much asseveration, I omit,
Of constancy henceforth till life should end.
When all this happened,—"What reward," cried she,
"For judging her Miranda by herself!
For never having entertained a thought
Of breaking promise, leaving home forsooth,

To follow who was fled to Portugal!
As if she thought they spoke a word of truth!
She knew what love was, knew that he loved her;
The Cousinry knew nothing of the kind."

I will not scandalize you and recount
How matters made the morning pass away.
Not one reproach, not one acknowledgment,
One explanation: all was understood!
Matters at end, the home-uneasiness
Cousins were feeling at this jaunt prolonged
Was ended also by the entry of—
Not simply him whose exit had been made
By mild command of doctor "Out with you!
I warrant we receive another man!"
But—would that I could say, the married pair!
And, quite another man assuredly,
Monsieur Léonce Miranda took on him
Forthwith to bid the trio, priest and nuns,
Constant in their attendance all this while,
Take his thanks and their own departure too;
Politely but emphatically. Next,
The Cousins were dismissed: "No protest, pray!
Whatever I engaged to do is done,
Or shall be—I but follow your advice:
Love I abjure: the lady, you behold,
Is changed as I myself; her sex is changed:
This is my Brother—He will tend me now,
Be all my world henceforth as brother should.
Gentlemen, of a kinship I revere,
Your interest in trade is laudable;
I purpose to indulge it: manage mine,
My goldsmith-business in the Place Vendôme,
Wholly—through purchase at the price adjudged
By experts I shall have assistance from.
If, in conformity with sage advice,
I leave a busy world of interests
I own myself unfit for—yours the care
That any world of other aims, wherein
I hope to dwell, be easy of access
Through ministration of the moneys due,
As we determine, with all proper speed,
Since I leave Paris to repair my health.
Say farewell to our Cousins, Brother mine!"

And, all submissiveness, as brother might,
The lady curtsied gracefully, and dropt
More than mere curtsey, a concluding phrase

So silver-soft, yet penetrative too,
That none of it escaped the favored ears:
"Had I but credited one syllable,
I should to-day be lying stretched on straw,
The produce of your miserable rente!
Whereas, I hold him—do you comprehend?"
Cousin regarded cousin, turned up eye,
And took departure, as our Tuscans laugh,
Each with his added palm-breadth of long nose,—
Curtailed but imperceptibly, next week,
When transfer was accomplished, and the trade
In Paris did indeed become their own,
But bought by them and sold by him on terms
'Twixt man and man,—might serve 'twixt wolf and wolf,
Substitute "bit and clawed" for "signed and sealed"—
Our ordinary business-terms, in short.
Another week, and Clairvaux broke in bloom
At end of April, to receive again
Monsieur Léonce Miranda, gentleman,
Ex-jeweller and goldsmith: never more—
According to the purpose he professed—
To quit this paradise, his property,
This Clara, his companion: so it proved.

The Cousins, each with elongated nose,
Discussed their bargain, reconciled them soon
To hard necessity, disbursed the cash,
And hastened to subjoin, wherever type
Proclaimed "Miranda" to the public, "Called
Now Firm-Miranda." There, a colony,
They flourish underneath the name that still
Maintains the old repute, I understand.
They built their Clairvaux, dream-Château, in Spain,
Perhaps—but Place Vendôme is waking worth:
Oh, they lost little!—only, man and man
Hardly conclude transactions of the kind
As cousin should with cousin,—cousins think.
For the rest, all was honorably done,
So, ere buds break to blossom, let us breathe!
Never suppose there was one particle
Of recrudescence—wound, half-healed before,
Set freshly running—sin, repressed as such,
New loosened as necessity of life!
In all this revocation and resolve,
Far be sin's self-indulgence from your thought!
The man had simply made discovery,
By process I respect if not admire,
That what was, was.—that turf, his feet had touched,

Felt solid just as much as yonder towers
He saw with eyes, but did not stand upon,
And could not, if he would, reach in a leap.
People had told him flowery turf was false
To footstep, tired the traveller soon, beside:
That was untrue. They told him "One fair stride
Plants on safe platform, and secures man rest."
That was untrue. Some varied the advice:
"Neither was solid, towers no more than turf:"
Double assertion, therefore twice as false.
"I like these amateurs"—our friend had laughed,
Could he turn what he felt to what he thought,
And, that again, to what he put in words:
"I like their pretty trial, proof of paste
Or precious stone, by delicate approach
Of eye askance, fine feel of finger-tip,
Or touch of tongue inquisitive for cold.
I tried my jewels in a crucible:
Fierce fire has felt them, licked them, left them sound.
Don't tell me that my earthly love is sham,
My heavenly fear a clever counterfeit!
Each may oppose each, yet be true alike!"

To build up, independent of the towers,
A durable pavilion o'er the turf,
Had issued in disaster. "What remained
Except, by tunnel, or else gallery,
To keep communication 'twixt the two,
Unite the opposites, both near and far,
And never try complete abandonment
Of one or other?" so he thought, not said.
And to such engineering feat, I say,
Monsieur Léonce Miranda saw the means
Precisely in this revocation prompt
Of just those benefits of worldly wealth
Conferred upon his Cousinry—all but!

This Clairvaux—you would know, were you at top
Of yonder crowning grace, its Belvedere—
Is situate in one angle-niche of three,
At equidistance from Saint-Rambert—there
Behind you, and The Ravissante, beside—
There: steeple, steeple, and this Clairvaux-top
(A sort of steeple) constitute a trine,
With not a tenement to break each side,
Two miles or so in length, if eye can judge.

Now this is native land of miracle.

Oh, why, why, why, from all recorded time,
Was miracle not wrought once, only once,
To help whoever wanted help indeed?
If on the day when Spring's green girlishness
Grew nubile, and she trembled into May,
And our Miranda climbed to clasp the Spring
A-tiptoe o'er the sea, those wafts of warmth,
Those cloudlets scudding under the bare blue,
And all that new sun, that fresh hope about
His airy place of observation,—friend,
Feel with me that if just then, just for once,
Some angel,—such as the authentic pen
Yonder records a daily visitant
Of ploughman Claude, rheumatic in the joints,
And spinster Jeanne, with megrim troubled sore,—
If such an angel, with naught else to do,
Had taken station on the pinnacle
And simply said, "Léonce, look straight before!
Neither to right hand nor to left: for why?
Being a stupid soul, you want a guide
To turn the goodness in you to account
And make stupidity submit itself.
Go to Saint-Rambert! Straightway get such guide!
There stands a man of men. You, jeweller,
Must needs have heard how once the biggest block
Of diamond now in Europe lay exposed
'Mid specimens of stone and earth and ore,
On huckster's stall,—Navona names the Square,
And Rome the city for the incident,—
Labelled 'quartz-crystal, price one halfpenny.'
Haste and secure that ha'p'worth, on your life!
That man will read you rightly head to foot,
Mark the brown face of you, the bushy beard,
The breadth 'twixt shoulderblades, and through each black
Castilian orbit, see into your soul.
Talk to him for five minutes—nonsense, sense,
No matter what—describe your horse, your hound,—
Give your opinion of the policy
Of Monsieur Rouher,—will he succor Rome?
Your estimate of what may outcome be
From Œcumenical Assemblage there!
After which samples of intelligence,
Rapidly run through those events you call
Your past life, tell what once you tried to do,
What you intend on doing this next May!
There he stands, reads an English newspaper,
Stock-still, and now, again upon the move,
Faces the beach to taste the spring, like you,

Since both are human beings in God's eye.
He will have understood you, I engage.
Endeavor, for your part, to understand
He knows more, and loves better, than the world
That never heard his name, and never may.
He will have recognized, ere breath be spent
And speech at end, how much that 's good in man,
And generous, and self-devoting, makes
Monsieur Léonce Miranda worth his help;
While sounding to the bottom ignorance
Historical and philosophical
And moral and religious, all one couch
Of crassitude, a portent of its kind.
Then, just as he would pityingly teach
Your body to repair maltreatment, give
Advice that you should make those stumps to stir
With artificial hands of caoutchouc,
So would he soon supply your crippled soul
With crutches, from his own intelligence,
Able to help you onward in the path
Of rectitude whereto your face is set,
And counsel justice—to yourself, the first,
To your associate, very like a wife
Or something better,—to the world at large,
Friends, strangers, horses, hounds, and Cousinry—
All which amount of justice will include
Justice to God. Go and consult his voice!"
Since angel would not say this simple truth,
What hinders that my heart relieve itself,
Milsand, who makest warm my wintry world,
And wise my heaven, if there we consort too?
Monsieur Léonce Miranda turned, alas,
Or was turned, by no angel, t' other way,
And got him guidance of The Ravissante.

Now, into the originals of faith,
Yours, mine, Miranda's, no inquiry here!
Of faith, as apprehended by mankind,
The causes, were they caught and catalogued,
Would too distract, too desperately foil
Inquirer. How may analyst reduce
Quantities to exact their opposites,
Value to zero, then bring zero back
To value of supreme preponderance?
How substitute thing meant for thing expressed?
Detect the wire-thread through that fluffy silk
Men call their rope, their real compulsive power?
Suppose effected such anatomy,

And demonstration made of what belief
Has moved believer—were the consequence
Reward at all? would each man straight deduce,
From proved reality of cause, effect
Conformable—believe and unbelieve
According to your True thus disengaged
From all his heap of False called reason first?

No: hand once used to hold a soft thick twist,
Cannot now grope its way by wire alone:
Childhood may catch the knack, scarce Youth, not Age!
That 's the reply rewards you. Just as well
Remonstrate to yon peasant in the blouse
That, had he justified the true intent
Of Nature who composed him thus and thus,
Weakly or strongly, here he would not stand
Struggling with uncongenial earth and sky,
But elsewhere tread the surface of the globe,
Since one meridian suits the faulty lungs,
Another bids the sluggish liver work.
"Here I was born, for better or for worse:
I did not choose a climate for myself;
Admit, my life were healthy, led elsewhere,"
(He answers,) "how am I to migrate, pray?"

Therefore the course to take is—spare your pains,
And trouble uselessly with discontent
Nor soul nor body, by parading proof
That neither haply had known ailment, placed
Precisely where the circumstance forbade
Their lot should fall to either of the pair.
But try and, what you find wrong, remedy,
Accepting the conditions: never ask
"How came you to be born here with those lungs,
That liver?" But bid asthma smoke a pipe,
Stramonium, just as if no Tropics were,
And ply with calomel the sluggish duct,
Nor taunt "The born Norwegian breeds no bile!"
And as with body, so proceed with soul:
Nor less discerningly, where faith you found,
However foolish and fantastic, grudge
To play the doctor and amend mistake,
Because a wisdom were conceivable
Whence faith had sprung robust above disease.
Far beyond human help, that source of things!
Since, in the first stage, so to speak,—first stare
Of apprehension at the invisible,—
Begins divergency of mind from mind,

Superior from inferior: leave this first!
Little you change there! What comes afterward—
From apprehended thing, each inference
With practicality concerning life,
This you may test and try, confirm the right
Or contravene the wrong which reasons there.
The offspring of the sickly faith must prove
Sickly act also: stop a monster-birth!
When water 's in the cup, and not the cloud,
Then is the proper time for chemic test:
Belief permits your skill to operate
When, drop by drop condensed from misty heaven,
'T is wrung out, lies a bowl-full in the fleece.
How dew by spoonfuls came, let Gideon say:
What purpose water serves, your word or two
May teach him, should he fancy it lights fire.

Concerning, then, our vaporous Ravissante—
How fable first precipitated faith.—
Silence you get upon such point from me.
But when I see come posting to the pair
At Clairvaux, for the cure of soul-disease,
This Father of the Mission, Parish-priest,
This Mother of the Convent, Nun I know—
They practise in that second stage of things;
They boast no fresh distillery of faith;
'T is dogma in the bottle, bright and old,
They bring; and I pretend to pharmacy.
They undertake the cure with all my heart!
He trusts them, and they surely trust themselves.
I ask no better. Never mind the cause,
Fons et origo of the malady:
Apply the drug with courage! Here 's our case.
Monsieur Léonce Miranda asks of God,
—May a man, living in illicit tie,
Continue, by connivance of the Church,
No matter what amends he please to make
Short of forthwith relinquishing the sin?
Physicians, what do you propose for cure?

Father and Mother of The Ravissante,
Read your own records, and you find prescribed
As follows, when a couple out of sorts
Rather than gravely suffering, sought your skill
And thereby got their health again. Perpend!
Two and a half good centuries ago,
Luc de la Maison Rouge, a nobleman
Of Claise, (the river gives this country name,)

And, just as noblewoman, Maude his wife,
Having been married many happy years
Spent in God's honor and man's service too,
Conceived, while yet in flower of youth and hope,
The project of departing each from each
Forever, and dissolving marriage-bonds
That both might enter a religious life.
Needing, before they came to such resolve,
Divine illumination,—course was clear,—
They visited your church in pilgrimage,
On Christmas morn: communicating straight,
They heard three Masses proper for the day,
"It is incredible with what effect"—
Quoth the Cistercian monk I copy from—
And, next day, came, again communicants,
Again heard Masses manifold, but now
With added thanks to Christ for special grace
And consolation granted: in the night,
Had been divorce from marriage, manifest
By signs and tokens. So, they made great gifts,
Left money for more Masses, and returned
Homeward rejoicing—he, to take the rules,
As Brother Dionysius, Capucin!
She, to become first postulant, then nun
According to the rules of Benedict,
Sister Scolastica: so ended they,
And so do I—not end nor yet commence
One note or comment. What was done was done.
Now, Father of the Mission, here 's your case!
And, Mother of the Convent, here 's its cure!
If separation was permissible,
And that decree of Christ "What God hath joined
Let no man put asunder" nullified
Because a couple, blameless in the world,
Had the conceit that, still more blamelessly,
Out of the world, by breach of marriage-vow,
Their life was like to pass,—you oracles
Of God,—since holy Paul says such you are,—
Hesitate, not one moment, to pronounce
When questioned by the pair now needing help,
"Each from the other go, you guilty ones,
Preliminary to your least approach
Nearer the Power that thus could strain a point
In favor of a pair of innocents
Who thought their wedded hands not clean enough
To touch and leave unsullied their souls' snow
Are not your hands found filthy by the world,
Mere human law and custom? Not a step

Nearer till hands be washed and purified!"

What they did say is immaterial, since
Certainly it was nothing of the kind.
There was no washing hands of him (alack,
You take me?—in the figurative sense!)
But, somehow, gloves were drawn o'er dirt and all,
And practice with the Church procured thereby.
Seeing that,—all remonstrance proved in vain,
Persuasives tried and terrors put to use,
I nowise question,—still the guilty pair
Only embraced the closelier, obstinate,—
Father and Mother went from Clairvaux back
Their weary way, with heaviness of heart,
I grant you, but each palm well crossed with coin,
And nothing like a smutch perceptible.
Monsieur Léonce Miranda might compound
For sin?—no, surely! but by gifts—prepare
His soul the better for contrition, say!

Gift followed upon gift, at all events.
Good counsel was rejected, on one part:
Hard money, on the other—may we hope
Was unreflectingly consigned to purse?

Two years did this experiment engage
Monsieur Léonce Miranda: how, by gifts
To God and to God's poor, a man might stay
In sin and yet stave off sin's punishment.
No salve could be conceived more nicely mixed
For this man's nature: generosity,—
Susceptibility to human ills,
Corporeal, mental,—self-devotedness
Made up Miranda—whether strong or weak
Elsewhere, may be inquired another time.
In mercy he was strong, at all events.
Enough! he could not see a beast in pain,
Much less a man, without the will to aid;
And where the will was, oft the means were too,
Since that good bargain with the Cousinry.

The news flew fast about the countryside
That, with the kind man, it was ask and have;
And ask and have they did. To instance you:—
A mob of beggars at The Ravissante
Clung to his skirts one day, and cried "We thirst!"
Forthwith he bade a cask of wine be broached
To satisfy all comers, till, dead-drunk

So satisfied, they strewed the holy place.
For this was grown religious and a rite:
Such slips of judgment, gifts irregular,
Showed but as spillings of the golden grist
On either side the hopper, through blind zeal;
Steadily the main stream went pouring on
From mill to mouth of sack—held wide and close
By Father of the Mission, Parish-priest,
And Mother of the Convent, Nun I know,
With such effect that, in the sequel, proof
Was tendered to the Court at Vire, last month,
That in these same two years, expenditure
At quiet Clairvaux rose to the amount
Of Forty Thousand English Pounds: whereof
A trifle went, no inappropriate close
Of bounty, to supply the Virgin's crown
With that stupendous jewel from New York,
Now blazing as befits the Star of Sea.

Such signs of grace, outward and visible,
I rather give you, for your sake and mine,
Than put in evidence the inward strife,
Spiritual effort to compound for fault
By payment of devotion—thank the phrase!
That payment was as punctual, do not doubt,
As its far easier fellow. Yesterday
I trudged the distance from The Ravissante
To Clairvaux, with my two feet: but our friend,
The more to edify the country-folk,
Was wont to make that journey on both knees.
"Maliciously perverted incident!"
Snarled the retort, when this was told at Vire:
"The man paid mere devotion as he passed,
Knelt decently at just each wayside shrine!"
Alas, my lawyer, I trudged yesterday—
On my two feet, and with both eyes wide ope,—
The distance, and could find no shrine at all!
According to his lights, I praise the man.
Enough! incessant was devotion, say—
With her, you know of, praying at his side.
Still, there be relaxations of the tense:
Or life indemnifies itself for strain,
Or finds its very strain grow feebleness.
Monsieur Léonce Miranda's days were passed
Much as of old, in simple work and play.
His first endeavor, on recovery
From that sad ineffectual sacrifice,
Had been to set about repairing loss:

Never admitting, loss was to repair.
No word at any time escaped his lips
—Betrayed a lurking presence, in his heart,
Of sorrow; no regret for mischief done—
Punishment suffered, he would rather say.
Good-tempered schoolboy-fashion, he preferred
To laugh away his flogging, fair price paid
For pleasure out of bounds: if needs must be,
Get pleasure and get flogged a second time!
A sullen subject would have nursed the scars
And made excuse, for throwing grammar by,
That bench was grown uneasy to the seat.
No: this poor fellow cheerfully got hands
Fit for his stumps, and what hands failed to do,
The other members did in their degree—
Unwonted service. With his mouth alone
He wrote, nay, painted pictures—think of that!
He played on a piano pedal-keyed,
Kicked out—if it was Bach's—good music thence.
He rode, that 's readily conceivable,
But then he shot and never missed his bird,
With other feats as dexterous: I infer
He was not ignorant what hands are worth,
When he resolved on ruining his own.
So the two years passed somehow—who shall say
Foolishly,—as one estimates mankind,
The work they do, the play they leave undone?—
Two whole years spent in that experiment
I told you of, at Clairvaux all the time,
From April on to April: why that month
More than another, notable in life?
Does the awakening of the year arouse
Man to new projects, nerve him for fresh feats
Of what proves, for the most part of mankind
Playing or working, novel folly too?
At any rate, I see no slightest sign
Of folly (let me tell you in advance),
Nothing but wisdom meets me manifest
In the procedure of the Twentieth Day
Of April, 'Seventy,—folly's year in France.

It was delightful Spring, and out of doors
Temptation to adventure. Walk or ride?
There was a wild young horse to exercise,
And teach the way to go, and pace to keep:
Monsieur Léonce Miranda chose to ride.
So, while they clapped soft saddle straight on back,
And bitted jaw to satisfaction,—since

The partner of his days must stay at home,
Teased by some trifling legacy of March
To throat or shoulder,—visit duly paid
And "farewell" given and received again,—
As chamber-door considerately closed
Behind him, still five minutes were to spend.
How better, than by clearing, two and two,
The staircase-steps and coming out aloft
Upon the platform yonder (raise your eyes!)
And tasting, just as those two years before,
Spring's bright advance upon the tower a-top,
The feature of the front, the Belvedere?

Look at it for a moment while I breathe.

IV

Ready to hear the rest? How good you are!

Now for this Twentieth splendid day of Spring,
All in a tale,—sun, wind, sky, earth and sea,—
To bid man, "Up, be doing!" Mount the stair,
Monsieur Léonce Miranda mounts so brisk,
And look—ere his elastic foot arrive—
Your longest, far and wide, o'er fronting space.
Yon white streak—Havre lighthouse! Name and name,
How the mind runs from each to each relay,
Town after town, till Paris' self be touched,
Superlatively big with life and death
To all the world, that very day perhaps!
He who stepped out upon the platform here,
Pinnacled over the expanse, gave thought
Neither to Rouher nor Ollivier, Roon
Nor Bismarck, Emperor nor King, but just
To steeple, church, and shrine, The Ravissante!

He saw Her, whom myself saw, but when Spring
Was passing into Fall: not robed and crowned
As, thanks to him, and her you know about,
She stands at present; but She smiled the same.
Thither he turned—to never turn away.

He thought ...

(Suppose I should prefer "He said"?
Along with every act—and speech is act—
There go, a multitude impalpable

To ordinary human faculty,
The thoughts which give the act significance.
Who is a poet needs must apprehend
Alike both speech and thoughts which prompt to speak.
Part these, and thought withdraws to poetry:
Speech is reported in the newspaper.)

He said, then, probably no word at all,
But thought as follows—in a minute's space—
One particle of ore beats out such leaf!

"This Spring-morn I am forty-three years old:
In prime of life, perfection of estate
Bodily, mental, nay, material too,—
My whole of worldly fortunes reach their height.
Body and soul alike on eminence:
It is not probable I ever raise
Soul above standard by increase of worth,
Nor reasonably may expect to lift
Body beyond the present altitude.

"Behold me, Lady called The Ravissante!
Such as I am,—gave myself to you
So long since, that I cannot say 'I give.'
All my belongings, what is summed in life,
I have submitted wholly—as man might,
At least, as I might, who am weak, not strong,—
Wholly, then, to your rule and governance,
So far as I had strength. My weakness was—
I felt a fascination, at each point
And pore of me, a Power as absolute
Claiming that soul should recognize her sway.
Oh, you were no whit clearlier Queen, I see,
Throughout the life that rolls out ribbon-like
Its shot-silk length behind me, than the strange
Mystery—how shall I denominate
The unrobed One? Robed you go and crowned as well,
Named by the nations: she is hard to name,
Though you have spelt out certain characters
Obscure upon what fillet binds her brow,
Lust of the flesh, lust of the eye, life's pride.
'So call her, and contemn the enchantress!'—'Crush
The despot, and recover liberty!'
Cried despot and enchantress at each ear.
You were conspicuous and pre-eminent,
Authoritative and imperial,—you
Spoke first, claimed homage: did I hesitate?
Born for no mastery, but servitude,

Men cannot serve two masters, says the Book;
Master should measure strength with master, then,
Before on servant is imposed a task.
You spoke first, promised best, and threatened most;
The other never threatened, promised, spoke
A single word, but, when your part was done,
Lifted a finger, and I, prostrate, knew
Films were about me, though you stood aloof
Smiling or frowning 'Where is power like mine
To punish or reward thee? Rise, thou fool!
Will to be free, and, lo, I lift thee loose!'
Did I not will, and could I rise a whit?
Lay I, at any time, content to lie?
'To lie, at all events, brings pleasure: make
Amends by undemanded pain!' I said.
Did not you prompt me? 'Purchase now by pain
Pleasure hereafter in the world to come!'
I could not pluck my heart out, as you bade:
Unbidden, I burned off my hands at least.
My soul retained its treasure; but my purse
Lightened itself with much alacrity.
Well, where is the reward? what promised fruit
Of sacrifice in peace, content? what sense
Of added strength to bear or to forbear?
What influx of new light assists me now
Even to guess you recognize a gain
In what was loss enough to mortal me?
But she, the less authoritative voice,
Oh, how distinct enunciating, how
Plain dealing! Gain she gave was gain indeed!
That, you deny: that, you contemptuous call
Acorns, swine's food not man's meat! 'Spurn the draff!'
Ay, but those life-tree apples I prefer,
Am I to die of hunger till they drop?
Husks keep flesh from starvation, anyhow.
Give those life-apples!—one, worth woods of oak,
Worth acorns by the wagon-load,—one shoot
Through heart and brain, assurance bright and brief
That you, my Lady, my own Ravissante,
Feel, through my famine, served and satisfied,
Own me, your starveling, soldier of a sort!
Your soldier! do I read my title clear
Even to call myself your friend, not foe?
What is the pact between us but a truce?
At best I shall have staved off enmity,
Obtained a respite, ransomed me from wrath.
I pay, instalment by instalment, life,
Earth's tribute-money, pleasures great and small,

Whereof should at the last one penny piece
Fall short, the whole heap becomes forfeiture.
You find in me deficient soldiership:
Want the whole life or none. I grudge that whole,
Because I am not sure of recompense:
Because I want faith. Whose the fault? I ask.
If insufficient faith have done thus much,
Contributed thus much of sacrifice,
More would move mountains, you are warrant. Well,
Grant, you, the grace, I give the gratitude!
And what were easier? 'Ask and have' folk call
Miranda's method: 'Have, nor need to ask!'
So do they formulate your quality
Superlative beyond my human grace.
The Ravissante, you ravish men away
From puny aches and petty pains, assuaged
By man's own art with small expenditure
Of pill or potion, unless, put to shame,
Nature is roused and sets things right herself.
Your miracles are grown our commonplace;
No day but pilgrim hobbles his last mile,
Kneels down and rises up, flings crutch away,
Or else appends it to the reverend heap
Beneath you, votive cripple-carpentry.
Some few meet failure—oh, they wanted faith,
And may betake themselves to La Salette,
Or seek Lourdes, so that hence the scandal limp!
The many get their grace and go their way
Rejoicing, with a tale to tell,—most like,
A staff to borrow, since the crutch is gone,
Should the first telling happen at my house,
And teller wet his whistle with my wine.
I tell this to a doctor and he laughs:
'Give me permission to cry—Out of bed,
You loth rheumatic sluggard! Cheat yon chair
Of laziness, its gouty occupant!—
You should see miracles performed! But now,
I give advice, and take as fee ten francs,
And do as much as does your Ravissante.
Send her that case of cancer to be cured
I have refused to treat for any fee,
Bring back my would-be patient sound and whole,
And see me laugh on t'other side my mouth!'
Can he be right, and are you hampered thus!
Such pettiness restricts a miracle
Wrought by the Great Physician, who hears prayer,
Visibly seated in your mother-lap!
He, out of nothing, made sky, earth, and sea,

And all that in them is, man, beast, bird, fish,
Down to this insect on my parapet.
Look how the marvel of a minim crawls!
Were I to kneel among the halt and maimed,
And pray 'Who mad'st the insect with ten legs,
Make me one finger grow where ten were once!'
The very priests would thrust me out of church.
'What folly does the madman dare expect?
No faith obtains—in this late age, at least—
Such cure as that! We ease rheumatics, though!'

"Ay, bring the early ages back again,
What prodigy were unattainable?
I read your annals. Here came Louis Onze,
Gave thrice the sum he ever gave before
At one time, some three hundred crowns, to wit—
On pilgrimage to pray for—health, he found?
Did he? I do not read it in Commines.
Here sent poor joyous Marie-Antoinette
To thank you that a Dauphin dignified
Her motherhood—called Duke of Normandy
And Martyr of the Temple, much the same
As if no robe of hers had dressed you rich;
No silver lamps, she gave, illume your shrine!
Here, following example, fifty years
Ago, in gratitude for birth again
Of yet another destined King of France,
Did not the Duchess fashion with her hands,
And frame in gold and crystal, and present
A bouquet made of artificial flowers?
And was he King of France, and is not he
Still Count of Chambord?

"Such the days of faith,
And such their produce to encourage mine!
What now, if I too count without my host?
I too have given money, ornament,
And 'artificial flowers'—which, when I plucked,
Seemed rooting at my heart and real enough:
What if I gain thereby nor health of mind,
Nor youth renewed which perished in its prime,
Burnt to a cinder 'twixt the red-hot bars,
Nor gain to see my second baby-hope
Of managing to live on terms with both
Opposing potentates, the Power and you,
Crowned with success? I dawdle out my days
In exile here at Clairvaux, with mock love,
That gives, while whispering 'Would I dared refuse! —

What the loud voice declares my heart's free gift!
Mock worship, mock superiority
O'er those I style the world's benighted ones,
That irreligious sort I pity so,
Dumas and even Hertford, who is Duke.

"Impiety? Not if I know myself!
Not if you know the heart and soul I bare,
I bid you cut, hack, slash, anatomize,
Till peccant part be found and flung away!
Demonstrate where I need more faith! Describe
What act shall evidence sufficiency
Of faith, your warrant for such exercise
Of power, in my behalf, as all the world,
Except poor praying me, declares profuse?
Poor me? It is that world, not me alone,
That world which prates of fixed laws and the like,
I fain would save, poor world so ignorant!
And your part were—what easy miracle?
Oh, Lady, could I make your want like mine!"

Then his face grew one luminosity.

"Simple, sufficient! Happiness at height!
I solve the riddle, I persuade mankind.
I have been just the simpleton who stands—
Summoned to claim his patrimonial rights—
At shilly-shally, may he knock or no
At his own door in his own house and home
Whereof he holds the very title-deeds!
Here is my title to this property,
This power you hold for profit of myself
And all the world at need—which need is now!

"My title—let me hear who controverts!
Count Mailleville built yon church. Why did he so?
Because he found your image. How came that?
His shepherd told him that a certain sheep
Was wont to scratch with hoof and scrape with horn
At ground where once the Danes had razed a church.
Thither he went, and there he dug, and thence
He disinterred the image he conveyed
In pomp to Londres yonder, his domain.
You liked the old place better than the new.
The Count might surely have divined as much:
He did not; some one might have spoke a word:
No one did. A mere dream had warned enough,
That back again in pomp you best were borne:

No dream warned, and no need of convoy was;
An angel caught you up and clapped you down,—
No mighty task; you stand one metre high,
And people carry you about at times.
Why, then, did you despise the simple course?
Because you are the Queen of Angels: when
You front us in a picture, there flock they,
Angels around you, here and everywhere.

"Therefore, to prove indubitable faith,
Those angels that acknowledge you their queen,
I summon them to bear me to your feet
From Clairvaux through the air, an easy trip!
Faith without flaw! I trust your potency,
Benevolence, your will to save the world—
By such a simplest of procedures, too!
Not even by affording angel-help,
Unless it please you: there 's a simpler mode:
Only suspend the law of gravity,
And, while at back, permitted to propel,
The air helps onward, let the air in front
Cease to oppose my passage through the midst!

"Thus I bestride the railing, leg o'er leg,
Thus, lo, I stand, a single inch away,
At dizzy edge of death,—no touch of fear,
As safe on tower above as turf below!
Your smile enswathes me in beatitude,
You lift along the votary—who vaults,
Who, in the twinkling of an eye, revives,
Dropt safely in the space before the church—
How crowded, since this morn is market-day!
I shall not need to speak. The news will run
Like wild-fire. 'Thousands saw Miranda's flight!'
'T is telegraphed to Paris in a trice.
The Boulevard is one buzz—'Do you believe?
Well, this time, thousands saw Miranda's flight:
You know him, goldsmith in the Place Vendôme.'
In goes the Empress to the Emperor:
'Now—will you hesitate to make disgorge
Your wicked King of Italy his gains,
Give the Legations to the Pope once more?'
Which done,—why, grace goes back to operate,
They themselves set a good example first,
Resign the empire twenty years usurped,
And Henry, the Desired One, reigns o'er France!
Regenerated France makes all things new!
My house no longer stands on Quai Rousseau,

But Quai rechristened Alacoque: a quai
Where Renan burns his book, and Veuillot burns
Renan beside, since Veuillot rules the roast,
Re-edits now indeed 'The Universe.'
O blessing, O superlatively big
With blessedness beyond all blessing dreamed
By man! for just that promise has effect,
'Old things shall pass away and all be new!'
Then, for a culminating mercy-feat,
Wherefore should I dare dream impossible
That I too have my portion in the change?
My past with all its sorrow, sin and shame,
Becomes a blank, a nothing! There she stands,
Clara de Millefleurs, all deodorized,
Twenty years' stain wiped off her innocence!
There never was Muhlhausen, nor at all
Duke Hertford: naught that was, remains, except
The beauty,—yes, the beauty is unchanged!
Well, and the soul too, that must keep the same!
And so the trembling little virgin hand
Melts into mine, that 's back again, of course!
—Think not I care about my poor old self!
I only want my hand for that one use,
To take her hand, and say 'I marry you—
Men, women, angels, you behold my wife!
There is no secret, nothing wicked here,
Nothing she does not wish the world to know!'
None of your married women have the right
To mutter 'Yes, indeed, she beats us all
In beauty,—but our lives are pure at least!'
Bear witness, for our marriage is no thing
Done in a corner! 'T is The Ravissante
Repairs the wrong of Paris. See, She smiles,
She beckons, She bids 'Hither, both of you!'
And may we kneel? And will you bless us both?
And may I worship you, and yet love her?
Then!"—
A sublime spring from the balustrade
About the tower so often talked about,
A flash in middle air, and stone-dead lay
Monsieur Léonce Miranda on the turf.

A gardener who watched, at work the while
Dibbling a flower-bed for geranium-shoots,
Saw the catastrophe, and, straightening back,
Stood up and shook his brows. "Poor soul, poor soul,
Just what I prophesied the end would be!
Ugh—the Red Night-cap!" (as he raised the head)

"This must be what he meant by those strange words
While I was weeding larkspurs, yesterday,
'Angels would take him!' Mad!"

No! sane, I say
Such being the conditions of his life,
Such end of life was not irrational.
Hold a belief, you only half-believe,
With all-momentous issues either way,—
And I advise you imitate this leap,
Put faith to proof, be cured or killed at once!
Call you men, killed through cutting cancer out,
The worse for such an act of bravery?
That 's more than I know. In my estimate,
Better lie prostrate on his turf at peace,
Than, wistful, eye, from out the tent, the tower,
Racked with a doubt, "Will going on bare knees
All the way to The Ravissante and back,
Saying my Ave Mary all the time,
Somewhat excuse if I postpone my march?
—Make due amends for that one kiss I gave
In gratitude to her who held me out
Superior Fricquot's sermon, hot from press,
A-spread with hands so sinful yet so smooth?"

And now, sincerely do I pray she stand,
Clara, with interposing sweep of robe,
Between us and this horror! Any screen
Turns white by contrast with the tragic pall;
And her dubiety distracts at least,
As well as snow, from such decided black.
With womanhood, at least, we have to do:
Ending with Clara—is the word too kind?

Let pass the shock! There 's poignancy enough
When what one parted with, a minute since,
Alive and happy, is returned a wreck—
All that was, all that seemed about to be,
Razed out and ruined now forevermore,
Because a straw descended on this scale
Rather than that, made death o'erbalance life.
But think of cage-mates in captivity,
Inured to day-long, night-long vigilance
Each of the other's tread and angry turn
If behind prison bars the jailer knocked:
These whom society shut out, and thus
Penned in, to settle down and regulate
By the strange law, the solitary life—

When death divorces such a fellowship,
Theirs may pair off with that prodigious woe
Imagined of a ghastly brotherhood—
One watcher left in lighthouse out at sea,
With leagues of surf between the land and him,
Alive with his dead partner on the rock;
One galley-slave, whom curse and blow compel
To labor on, ply oar—beside his chain,
Encumbered with a corpse-companion now.
Such these: although, no prisoners, self-entrenched,
They kept the world off from their barricade.

Memory, gratitude, was poignant, sure,
Though pride brought consolation of a kind.
Twenty years long had Clara been—of whom
The rival, nay, the victor, past dispute?
What if in turn The Ravissante at length
Proved victor—which was doubtful—anyhow,
Here lay the inconstant with, conspicuous too,
The fruit of his good fortune!

"Has he gained
By leaving me?" she might soliloquize:
"All love could do, I did for him. I learned
By heart his nature, what he loved and loathed.
Leaned to with liking, turned from with distaste.
No matter what his least velleity,
I was determined he should want no wish,
And in conformity administered
To his requirement; most of joy I mixed
With least of sorrow in life's daily draught,
Twenty years long, life's proper average.
And when he got to quarrel with my cup,
Would needs out-sweeten honey, and discard
That gall-drop we require lest nectar cloy,—
I did not call him fool, and vex my friend,
But quietly allowed experiment,
Encouraged him to spice his drink, and now
Grate lignum vitæ" now bruise so-called grains
Of Paradise, and pour now, for perfume,
Distilment rare, the rose of Jericho,
Holy-thorn, passion-flower, and what know I?
Till beverage obtained the fancied smack.
'T was wild-flower-wine that neither helped nor harmed
Who sipped and held it for restorative—
What harm? But here has he been through the hedge
Straying in search of simples, while my back
Was turned a minute, and he finds a prize,

Monkshood and belladonna! O my child,
My truant little boy, despite the beard,
The body two feet broad and six feet long,
And what the calendar counts middle age—
You wanted, did you, to enjoy a flight?
Why not have taken into confidence
Me, that was mother to you?—never mind
What mock disguise of mistress held you mine!
Had you come laughing, crying, with request,
'Make me fly, mother!' I had run upstairs
And held you tight the while I danced you high
In air from tower-top, singing 'Off we go
(On pilgrimage to Lourdes some day next month),
And swift we soar (to Rome with Peter-pence),
And low we light (at Paris where we pick
Another jewel from our store of stones
And send it for a present to the Pope)!'
So, dropt indeed you were, but on my knees,
Rolling and crowing, not a whit the worse
For journey to your Ravissante and back.
Now, no more Clairvaux—which I made you build,
And think an inspiration of your own—
No more fine house, trim garden, pretty park,
Nothing I used to busy you about,
And make believe you worked for my surprise!
What weariness to me will work become
Now that I need not seem surprised again!
This boudoir, for example, with the doves
(My stupid maid has damaged, dusting one)
Embossed in stucco o'er the looking-glass
Beside the toilet-table! dear—dear me!"

Here she looked up from her absorbing grief,
And round her, crow-like grouped, the Cousinry,
(She grew aware) sat witnesses at watch.
For, two days had elapsed since fate befell
The courser in the meadow, stretched so stark.
They did not cluster on the tree-tops, close
Their sooty ranks, caw and confabulate
For nothing: but, like calm determined crows,
They came to take possession of their corpse.
And who shall blame them? Had not they the right?
One spoke. "They would be gentle, not austere.
They understood, and were compassionate.
Madame Muhlhausen lay too abject now
For aught but the sincerest pity; still,
Since plain speech salves the wound it seems to make,
They must speak plainly—circumstances spoke!

Sin had conceived and brought forth death indeed.
As the commencement, so the close of things:
Just what might be expected all along!
Monsieur Léonce Miranda launched his youth
Into a cesspool of debauchery,
And, if he thence emerged all dripping slime,
—Where was the change except from thin to thick,
One warm rich mud-bath, Madame?—you, in place
Of Paris-drainage and distilment, you
He never needed budge from, boiled to rags!
True, some good instinct left the natural man,
Some touch of that deep dye wherewith imbued
By education, in his happier day,
The hopeful offspring of high parentage
Was fleece-marked moral and religious sheep,—
Some ruddle, faint reminder (we admit),
Stuck to Miranda, rubbed he ne'er so rude
Against the goatly coarseness: to the last,
Moral he styled himself, religious too!
Which means—what ineradicable good
You found, you never left till good's self proved
Perversion and distortion, nursed to growth
So monstrous, that the tree-stock, dead and dry,
Were seemlier far than such a heap grotesque
Of fungous nourishing excrescence. Here,
Sap-like affection, meant for family,
Stole off to feed one sucker fat—yourself;
While branchage, trained religiously aloft
To rear its head in reverence to the sun,
Was pulled down earthward, pegged and picketed,
By topiary contrivance, till the tree
Became an arbor where, at vulgar ease,
Sat superstition grinning through the loops.
Still, nature is too strong or else too weak
For cockney treatment: either, tree springs back
To pristine shape, or else degraded droops,
And turns to touchwood at the heart. So here—
Body and mind, at last the man gave way.
His body—there it lies, what part was left
Unmutilated! for, the strife commenced
Two years ago, when, both hands burnt to ash,
—A branch broke loose, by loss of what choice twigs!
As for his mind—behold our register
Of all its moods, from the incipient mad,
Nay, mere erratic, to the stark insane,
Absolute idiocy or what is worse!
All have we catalogued—extravagance
In worldly matters, luxury absurd,

And zeal as crazed in its expenditure
Of nonsense called devotion. Don't we know
—We Cousins, bound in duty to our kin,—
What mummeries were practised by you two
At Clairvaux? Not a servant got discharge
But came and told his grievance, testified
To acts which turn religion to a farce.
And as the private mock, so patent—see—
The public scandal! Ask the neighborhood—
Or rather, since we asked them long ago,
Read what they answer, depositions down,
Signed, sealed and sworn to! Brief, the man was mad.
We are his heirs and claim our heritage.
Madame Muhlhausen,—whom good taste forbids
We qualify as do these documents,—
Fear not lest justice stifle mercy's prayer!
True, had you lent a willing ear at first,
Had you obeyed our call two years ago,
Restrained a certain insolence of eye,
A volubility of tongue, that time,
Your prospects had been none the worse, perhaps.
Still, fear not but a decent competence
Shall smooth the way for your declining age!
What we propose, then" ...

Clara dried her eyes,
Sat up, surveyed the consistory, spoke
After due pause, with something of a smile.

"Gentlemen, kinsfolk of my friend defunct,
In thus addressing me—of all the world!—
You much misapprehend what part I play.
I claim no property you speak about.
You might as well address the park-keeper,
Harangue him on some plan advisable
For covering the park with cottage-plots.
He is the servant, no proprietor,
His business is to see the sward kept trim,
Untrespassed over by the indiscreet:
Beyond that, he refers you to myself—
Another servant of another kind—
Who again—quite as limited in act—
Refer you, with your projects,—can I else?
To who in mastery is ultimate,
The Church. The Church is sole administrant,
Since sole possessor of what worldly wealth
Monsieur Léonce Miranda late possessed.
Often enough has he attempted, nay,

Forced me, wellnigh, to occupy the post
You seemingly suppose I fill,—receive
As gift the wealth intrusted me as grace.
This—for quite other reasons than appear
So cogent to your perspicacity—
This I refused; and, firm as you could wish,
Still was my answer, 'We two understand
Each one the other. I am intimate
—As how can be mere fools and knaves—or, say,
Even your Cousins?—with your love to me,
Devotion to the Church. Would Providence
Appoint, and make me certain of the same,
That I survive you (which is little like,
Seeing you hardly overpass my age
And more than match me in abundant health)
In such case, certainly I would accept
Your bounty: better I than alien hearts
Should execute your planned benevolence
To man, your proposed largess to the Church,
But though I be survivor,—weakly frame,
With only woman's wit to make amends,—
When I shall die, or while I am alive,
Cannot you figure me an easy mark
For hypocritical rapacity,
Kith, kin and generation, crouching low,
Ever on the alert to pounce on prey?
Far be it I should say they profited
By that first frenzy-fit themselves induced,—
Cold-blooded scenical buffoons at sport
With horror and damnation o'er a grave:
That were too shocking—I absolve them there!
Nor did they seize the moment of your swoon
To rifle pocket, wring a paper thence,
Their Cousinly dictation, and enrich
Thereby each mother's son as heart could wish,
Had nobody supplied a codicil.
But when the pain, poor friend! had prostrated
Your body, though your soul was right once more,
I fear they turned your weakness to account!
Why else to me, who agonizing watched,
Sneak, cap in hand, now bribe me to forsake
My maimed Léonce, now bully, cap on head,
The impudent pretension to assuage
Such sorrows as demanded Cousins' care?—
For you rejected, hated, fled me, far
In foreign lands you laughed at me!—they judged.
And, think you, will the unkind one hesitate
To try conclusions with my helplessness,—

To pounce on and misuse your derelict,
Helped by advantage that bereavement lends
Folk, who, while yet you lived, played tricks like these?
You only have to die, and they detect,
In all you said and did, insanity!
Your faith was fetish-worship, your regard
For Christ's prime precept which endows the poor
And strips the rich, a craze from first to last!
They so would limn your likeness, paint your life,
That if it ended by some accident,—
For instance, if, attempting to arrange
The plants below that dangerous Belvedere
I cannot warn you from sufficiently,
You lost your balance and fell headlong—fine
Occasion, such, for crying Suicide!
Non compos mentis, naturally next,
Hands over Clairvaux to a Cousin-tribe
Who nor like me nor love The Ravissante:
Therefore be ruled by both! Life-interest
In Clairvaux,—conservation, guardianship
Of earthly good for heavenly purpose,—give
Such and no other proof of confidence!
Let Clara represent The Ravissante!'
—To whom accordingly, he then and there
Bequeathed each stick and stone, by testament
In holograph, mouth managing the quill:
Go, see the same in Londres, if you doubt!"

Then smile grew laugh, as sudden up she stood
And out she spoke: intemperate the speech!

"And now, sirs, for your special courtesy,
Your candle held up to the character
Of Lucie Steiner, whom you qualify
As coming short of perfect womanhood.
Yes, kindly critics, truth for once you tell!
True is it that through childhood, poverty,
Sloth, pressure of temptation, I succumbed,
And, ere I found what honor meant, lost mine.
So was the sheep lost, which the Shepherd found
And never lost again. My friend found me;
Or better say, the Shepherd found us both—
Since he, my friend, was much in the same mire,
When first we made acquaintance. Each helped each,—
A twofold extrication from the slough;
And, saving me, he saved himself. Since then,
Unsmirched we kept our cleanliness of coat.
It is his perfect constancy, you call

My friend's main fault—he never left his love!
While as for me, I dare your worst, impute
One breach of loving bond, these twenty years.
To me whom only cobwebs bound, you count!
'He was religiously disposed in youth!'
That may be, though we did not meet at church.
Under my teaching did he, like you scamps,
Become Voltairian—fools who mock his faith?
'Infirm of body!' I am silent there:
Even yourselves acknowledge service done,
Whatever motive your own souls supply
As inspiration. Love made labor light."

Then laugh grew frown, and frown grew terrible.
Do recollect what sort of person shrieked—
"Such was I, saint or sinner, what you please:
And who is it casts stone at me but you?
By your own showing, sirs, you bought and sold,
Took what advantage bargain promised bag,
Abundantly did business, and with whom?
The man whom you pronounce imbecile, push
Indignantly aside if he presume
To settle his affairs like other folk!
How is it you have stepped into his shoes,
And stand there, bold as brass, 'Miranda, late;
Now, Firm-Miranda'? Sane, he signed away
That little birthright, did he? Hence to trade!
I know and he knew who 't was dipped and ducked,
Truckled and played the parasite in vain,
As now one, now the other, here you cringed,
Were feasted, took our presents, you—those drops,
Just for your wife's adornment! you—that spray
Exactly suiting, as most diamonds would,
Your daughter on her marriage! No word then
Of somebody the wanton! Hence, I say,
Subscribers to the 'Siècle,' every snob—
For here the post brings me the 'Univers'!
Home and make money in the Place Vendôme,
Sully yourselves no longer by my sight,
And, when next Schneider wants a new parure,
Be careful lest you stick there by mischance
That stone beyond compare intrusted you
To kindle faith with, when, Miranda's gift,
Crowning the very crown, The Ravissante
Shall claim it! As to Clairvaux—talk to Her!
She answers by the Chapter of Raimbaux!"
Vituperative, truly! All this wrath
Because the man's relations thought him mad!

Whereat, I hope you see the Cousinry
Turn each to other, blankly dolorous,
Consult a moment, more by shrug and shrug
Than mere man's language,—finally conclude
To leave the reprobate untroubled now
In her unholy triumph, till the Law
Shall right the injured ones; for gentlemen
Allow the female sex, this sort at least.
Its privilege. So, simply "Cockatrice!"—
"Jezebel!"—"Queen of the Camellias!"—cried
Cousin to cousin, as yon hinge a-creak
Shut out the party, and the gate returned
To custody of Clairvaux. "Pretty place!
What say you, when it proves our property,
To trying a concurrence with La Roche,
And laying down a rival oyster-bed?
Where the park ends, the sea begins, you know."
So took they comfort till they came to Vire.

But I would linger, fain to snatch a look
At Clara as she stands in pride of place,
Somewhat more satisfying than my glance
So furtive, so near futile, yesterday,
Because one must be courteous. Of the masks
That figure in this little history,
She only has a claim to my respect,
And one-eyed, in her French phrase, rules the blind.
Miranda hardly did his best with life:
He might have opened eye, exerted brain,
Attained conception as to right and law
In certain points respecting intercourse
Of man with woman—love, one likes to say;
Which knowledge had dealt rudely with the claim
Of Clara to play representative
And from perdition rescue soul, forsooth!
Also, the sense of him should have sufficed
For building up some better theory
Of how God operates in heaven and earth,
Than would establish Him participant
In doings yonder at The Ravissante.
The heart was wise according to its lights
And limits; but the head refused more sun,
And shrank into its mew, and craved less space.
Clara, I hold the happier specimen,—
It may be, through that artist-preference
For work complete, inferiorly proposed,
To incompletion, though it aim aright.
Morally, no! Aspire, break bounds! I say,

Endeavor to be good, and better still,
And best! Success is naught, endeavor 's all.
But intellect adjusts the means to ends,
Tries the low thing, and leaves it done, at least;
No prejudice to high thing, intellect
Would do and will do, only give the means.
Miranda, in my picture-gallery,
Presents a Blake; be Clara—Meissonnier!
Merely considered so by artist, mind!
For, break through Art and rise to poetry,
Bring Art to tremble nearer, touch enough
The verge of vastness to inform our soul
What orb makes transit through the dark above,
And there 's the triumph!—there the incomplete,
More than completion, matches the immense,—
Then, Michelagnolo against the world!
With this proviso, let me study her
Approvingly, the finished little piece!
Born, bred, with just one instinct,—that of growth,—
Her quality was, caterpillar-like,
To all-unerringly select a leaf
And without intermission feed her fill,
Become the Painted Peacock, or belike
The Brimstone-wing, when time of year should suit;
And 't is a sign (say entomologists)
Of sickness, when the creature stops its meal
One minute, either to look up at heaven,
Or turn aside for change of aliment.
No doubt there was a certain ugliness
In the beginning, as the grub grew worm:
She could not find the proper plant at once,
But crawled and fumbled through a whole parterre.
Husband Muhlhausen served for stuff not long:
Then came confusion of the slimy track
From London, "where she gave the tone awhile,"
To Paris: let the stalks start up again,
Now she is off them, all the greener they!
But, settled on Miranda, how she sucked,
Assimilated juices, took the tint,
Mimicked the form and texture of her food!
Was he for pastime? Who so frolic-fond
As Clara? Had he a devotion-fit?
Clara grew serious with like qualm, be sure!
In health and strength he,—healthy too and strong,
She danced, rode, drove, took pistol-practice, fished,
Nay, "managed sea-skiff with consummate skill."
In pain and weakness, he,—she patient watched
And whiled the slow drip-dropping hours away.

She bound again the broken self-respect,
She picked out the true meaning from mistake,
Praised effort in each stumble, laughed "Well climbed!"
When others groaned "None ever grovelled so!"
"Rise, you have gained experience!" was her word:
"Lie satisfied, the ground is just your place!"
They thought appropriate counsel. "Live, not die,
And take my full life to eke out your own:
That shall repay me and with interest!
Write!—is your mouth not clever as my hand?
Paint!—the last Exposition warrants me,
Plenty of people must ply brush with toes.
And as for music—look, what folk nickname
A lyre, those ancients played to ravishment,—
Over the pendule, see, Apollo grasps
A three-stringed gimcrack which no Liszt could coax
Such music from as jew's-harp makes to-day!
Do your endeavor like a man, and leave
The rest to 'fortune who assists the bold'—
Learn, you, the Latin which you taught me first,
You clever creature—clever, yes, I say!"

If he smiled "Let us love, love's wrong comes right,
Shows reason last of all! Necessity
Must meanwhile serve for plea—so, mind not much
Old Fricquot's menace!"—back she smiled "Who minds?"
If he sighed "Ah, but She is strict, they say,
For all Her mercy at The Ravissante,
She scarce will be put off so!"—straight a sigh
Returned "My lace must go to trim Her gown!"
I nowise doubt she inwardly believed
Smiling and sighing had the same effect
Upon the venerated image. What
She did believe in, I as little doubt,
Was—Clara's self's own birthright to sustain
Existence, grow from grub to butterfly,
Upon unlimited Miranda-leaf;
In which prime article of faith confirmed,
According to capacity, she fed
On and on till the leaf was eaten up,
That April morning. Even then, I praise
Her forethought which prevented leafless stalk
Bestowing any hoarded succulence
On earwig and black-beetle squat beneath;—
Clairvaux, that stalk whereto her hermitage
She tacked by golden throw of silk, so fine,
So anything but feeble, that her sleep
inside it, through last winter, two years long,

Recked little of the storm and strife without.
"But—loved him?" Friend, I do not praise her love!
True love works never for the loved one so,
Nor spares skin-surface, smoothening truth away.
Love bids touch truth, endure truth, and embrace
Truth, though, embracing truth, love crush itself.
"Worship not me, but God!" the angels urge:
That is love's grandeur: still, in pettier love
The nice eye can distinguish grade and grade.
Shall mine degrade the velvet green and puce
Of caterpillar, palmer-worm—or what—
Ball in and out of ball, each ball with brush
Of Venus' eye-fringe round the turquoise egg
That nestles soft,—compare such paragon
With any scarabæus of the brood
Which, born to fly, keeps wing in wing-case, walks
Persistently a-trundling dung on earth?

Egypt may venerate such hierophants,
Not I—the couple yonder, Father Priest
And Mother Nun, who came and went and came,
Beset this Clairvaux, trundled money-muck
To midden and the main heap oft enough,
But never bade unshut from sheath the gauze,
Nor showed that, who would fly, must let fall filth,
And warn "Your jewel, brother, is a blotch:
Sister, your lace trails ordure! Leave your sins,
And so best gift with Crown and grace with Robe!"

The superstition is extinct, you hope?
It were, with my good will! Suppose it so,
Bethink you likewise of the latest use
Whereto a Night-cap is convertible,
And draw your very thickest, thread and thrum,
O'er such a decomposing face of things,
Once so alive, it seemed immortal too!

This happened two years since. The Cousinry
Returned to Paris, called in help from Law,
And in due form proceeded to dispute
Monsieur Léonce Miranda's competence,
Being insane, to make a valid Will.

Much testimony volunteered itself;
The issue hardly could be doubtful—but
For that sad 'Seventy which must intervene,
Provide poor France with other work to mind
Than settling lawsuits, even for the sake

Of such a party as The Ravissante.
It only was this Summer that the case
Could come and be disposed of, two weeks since,
At Vire—Tribunal Civil—Chamber First.

Here, issued with all regularity,
I hold the judgment—just, inevitable,
Nowise to be contested by what few
Can judge the judges; sum and substance, thus:—

"Inasmuch as we find, the Cousinry,
During that very period when they take
Monsieur Léonce Miranda for stark mad,
Considered him to be quite sane enough
For doing much important business with—
Nor showed suspicion of his competence
Until, by turning of the tables, loss
Instead of gain accrued to them thereby,—
Plea of incompetence we set aside.

—"The rather, that the dispositions, sought
To be impugned, are natural and right,
Nor jar with any reasonable claim
Of kindred, friendship, or acquaintance here.
Nobody is despoiled, none overlooked;
Since the testator leaves his property
To just that person whom, of all the world,
He counted he was most indebted to.
In mere discharge, then, of conspicuous debt,
Madame Muhlhausen has priority,
Enjoys the usufruct of Clairvaux.

"Next,
Such debt discharged, such life determining,
Such earthly interest provided for,
Monsieur Léonce Miranda may bequeath,
In absence of more fit recipient, fund
And usufruct together to the Church
Whereof he was a special devotee.

"—Which disposition, being consonant
With a long series of such acts and deeds
Notorious in his lifetime, needs must stand,
Unprejudiced by eccentricity
Nowise amounting to distemper: since,
In every instance signalized as such,
We recognize no overleaping bounds,
No straying out of the permissible!

Duty to the Religion of the Land,—
Neither excessive nor inordinate.

"The minor accusations are dismissed;
They prove mere freak and fancy, boyish mood
In age mature of simple kindly man.
Exuberant in generosities
To all the world: no fact confirms the fear
He meditated mischief to himself
That morning when he met the accident
Which ended fatally. The case is closed."

How otherwise? So, when I grazed the skirts,
And had the glimpse of who made, yesterday,—
Woman and retinue of goats and sheep,—
The sombre path one whiteness, vision-like,
As out of gate, and in at gate again,
They wavered,—she was lady there for life:
And, after life—I hope, a white success
Of some sort, wheresoever life resume
School interrupted by vacation—death;
Seeing that home she goes with prize in hand,
Confirmed the Châtelaine of Clairvaux.

True,
Such prize fades soon to insignificance.
Though she have eaten her Miranda up,
And spun a cradle-cone through, which she pricks
Her passage, and proves peacock-butterfly,
This Autumn—wait a little week of cold!
Peacock and death's-head-moth end much the same.
And could she still continue spinning,—sure,
Cradle would soon crave shroud for substitute,
And o'er this life of hers distaste would drop
Red-cotton-Nightcap-wise.

How say you, friend?
Have I redeemed my promise? Smile assent
Through the dark Winter-gloom between us both!
Already, months ago and miles away,
I just as good as told you, in a flash,
The while we paced the sands before my house,
All this poor story—truth and nothing else.
Accept that moment's flashing, amplified,
Impalpability reduced to speech,
Conception proved by birth,—no other change!
Can what Saint-Rambert flashed me in a thought,

Good gloomy London make a poem of?
Such ought to be whatever dares precede,
Play ruddy herald-star to your white blaze
About to bring us day. How fail imbibe
Some foretaste of effulgence? Sun shall wax,
And star shall wane: what matter, so star tell
The drowsy world to start awake, rub eyes,
And stand all ready for morn's joy a-blush?

Robert Browning – A Short Biography

He is the equal of any Victorian Poet that could be mentioned. However, Browning continues to be in the shadow of Tennyson, Arnold, Hopkins, Morris and many others.

Robert Browning was born on May 7th, 1812 in Walworth in the parish of Camberwell, London. He was baptized on June 14th, 1812, at Lock's Fields Independent Chapel, York Street, Walworth.

Browning's early years were certainly very interesting. His mother was an excellent pianist and a very devout evangelical Christian. His father, who worked as a clerk at the Bank of England, was also an artist, scholar, antiquarian, and collector of books and pictures. Indeed, he amassed more than 6,000 volumes of rare books including works in Greek, Hebrew, Latin, French, Italian, and Spanish. For the young and curious Browning, it was a wonderful resource, added to which his father was a guiding force in his education.

Many accounts attest that Browning was already proficient at reading and writing by the age of five. He is said to have been a bright but anxious student and to have studied and learnt Latin, Greek, and French by the time he was fourteen. From fourteen to sixteen he was educated at home, tutored in music, drawing, dancing, and horsemanship. Certainly, language and the arts were two areas the young Browning both absorbed and pushed himself towards.

At the age of twelve he wrote a volume of Byronic verse he called Incondita, which his parents attempted to have published. The attempts were unsuccessful and, disappointed, Browning destroyed the work.

In 1825, a cousin gave Browning a collection of Percy Bysshe Shelley's poetry; Browning was so enamored with the poems that he asked for the rest of Shelley's works for his thirteenth birthday. In fact, Browning then went the extra mile, declaring himself to be both a vegetarian and an atheist in honour of his hero.

Intriguingly it seems that the rejection of his first volume didn't dim his appreciation of other poets, but it appears to have stopped him writing any poems between the ages of thirteen and twenty.

In 1828, Browning enrolled at the newly-opened University of London. He was uncomfortable with the experience and he soon left, anxious to read and absorb at his own pace.

His education which, overall is notably rambling and lacks a structure that many of his artistic contemporaries enjoyed, i.e. excellent public schooling and then a degree at Oxford or Cambridge, may present many of his critics with ammunition to criticize, but alternatively his hap-hazard education certainly contributed to many of the references that baffled both critics and his audience, but they tellingly show the breath and scale of what he could turn words too. What others would call obscure references were, to Browning, remarkably obvious.

Browning's early career was very promising. His long poem Pauline (of which only a fragment was ever finished and published) brought him to the attention of the Pre-Raphaelite master Dante Gabriel Rossetti and his difficult Paracelsus (published in 1835) was warmly admired by both Dickens and Wordsworth.

In the 1830s he met the actor William Macready and was encouraged to develop and turn his talents to the stage by writing verse drama. But these plays, including Strafford, which ran for five nights in 1837, and those contained within the Bells and Pomegranates series, were, for the most part, unsuccessful.

During this period Browning began to discover that his real talents lay in taking a single character and allowing that character to discover more about himself by revealing further personal aspects of himself in his speeches; the dramatic monologue. The techniques he developed through this—especially the use of diction, rhythm, and symbol—are regarded as his most important contribution to poetry. They would later influence such major poets of the 20th Century as Ezra Pound, T. S. Eliot, and Robert Frost.

By 1840, with the publication of Sordello, the tide turned somewhat. Many thought he was being deliberately obscure, opaque beyond measure and his poetry for the next decade or so was not eagerly acquired or talked about.

As Browning attempted to rehabilitate his career he began a relationship with Elizabeth Barrett in 1845. He had read her poems and, being totally charmed by their quality, was determined to meet her. The poetess was better known than the younger Browning but suffered from a debilitating illness and was also subject to the harsh behaviour of her over-bearing father. Nevertheless, the new couple were soon inseparable.

Her father, as he did with any of his children that married, disinherited her. Despite this she had some money from her own resources and sensing that the best outcome for both the relationship and her own health was to move abroad the couple did just that. After a private marriage at St Marylebone Parish Church, in September 1846, they journeyed to Europe to honeymoon in Paris.

Their new life now took them to Italy, first to Pisa and a little later to Florence. There they absorbed life and one another.

But in the short term the literary assault on Browning's work did not let up. He was now criticized by such patrician writers as Charles Kingsley for his abandonment of England for foreign lands. Browning could do little to answer these attacks except to compose with his pen and continue with his poetical journey.

The Browning's were well respected, and even famous. Elizabeth health began to improve, she grew stronger and in 1849, at the age of 43, between four miscarriages, she gave birth to a son, Robert Wiedeman Barrett Browning, whom they nicknamed "Penini" or "Pen",

Intriguingly despite his growing reputation and return to form as a poet he was more often than not known as 'Elizabeth Barrett's husband'.

Work flowed from his pen that was to ensure his reputation as one of England's leading poets. When his collection Men and Women was published in 1855 it contained some of his finest lines. It was dedicated to Elizabeth. Life had begun to smile handsome rewards upon the Brownings.

Victorian society was very much taken with all things spiritualist. It was not enough to have command of much of the globe through Empire, they wished to know and explore wherever they could. The spirit world beckoned their interest. Browning dissented from this view believing it was all a hoax and a fraud. Elizabeth, however, was inclined to believe and this caused several disagreements between the couple.

They attended a séance by Daniel Dunglas Home, in July 1855. (Home was a famous and clamored after Scottish physical medium with the reported ability to levitate and speak with the dead). It is said that during this séance a spirit face materialised. Home then claimed it was the face of Browning's son who had died in infancy. Browning seized the 'materialisation' which turned out to be Home's bare foot. Browning had never lost a son in infancy.

After the séance, Browning wrote an angry letter to The Times, in which he said: "the whole display of hands, spirit utterances etc., was a cheat and imposture."

The Browning's time in Italy were immensely rewarding years for both their personal and professional lives. Browning encouraged her to include Sonnets from the Portuguese in her published works, these beautiful poems are undoubtedly one of the highlights of English love poetry.

Elizabeth had become quite politicised during these years. Engrossed in Italian politics (which was continuing to slowly re-unify the country), she issued a small volume of political poems entitled Poems before Congress (1860) most of which were written to express her sympathy with the Italian cause after the earlier outbreak of The Second Italian Independence War in 1859. In England they caused uproar. Conservative magazines such as Blackwood's and the Saturday Review labelled her a fanatic. She dedicated the book to her husband.

But in 1861 tragedy struck.

The couple had spent the winter of 1860–61 in Rome when Elizabeth's health deteriorated again and they returned to Florence in early June. However, these turned out to be her final weeks. Only morphine would now still the pain. She died in Browning's arms on June 29th, 1861. Browning said that she died "smilingly, happily, and with a face like a girl's .... Her last word was .... "Beautiful".

Her burial took place in the nearby Protestant English Cemetery of Florence. The local people were deeply saddened, and shops closed their doors in grief and respect.

Browning and their son were obviously devastated. Unable to bear being in Florence without Elizabeth they soon returned to London to live at 19 Warwick Crescent, Maida Vale.

As he re integrated himself back into the London literary scene he began to finally receive the proper praise, respect and reputation that his works deserved.

Browning went on to publish Dramatis Personæ (1864), and The Ring and the Book (1868–1869). The latter, based on an "old yellow book" which told of a seventeenth-century Italian murder trial, received wide and generous critical acclaim. Although by now he was in the twilight of a long and prolific career, that had achieved some notable ups and downs, he was respected and indeed renowned for his talents and works.

In 1878, he revisited Italy for the first time since Elizabeth's death. He would return there on several further occasions but never to Florence.

Such was the esteem he was held in that The Browning Society was founded in 1881. Although he had never obtained a degree (something that set him apart from many other Victorian poets) he was now awarded honorary degrees from Oxford University in 1882 and then the University of Edinburgh in 1884.

In 1887, Browning produced the major work of his later years, Parleyings with Certain People of Importance in Their Day. Browning now spoke with his own voice as he engaged in a series of dialogues with long-forgotten figures of literary, artistic, and philosophic history. Unfortunately, both the critics and public were completely baffled by this.

On April 7th, 1889 Browning attended a dinner party at the home of his friend, the artist Rudolf Lehmann. The highlight of which was a recording made on a wax cylinder on an Edison cylinder phonograph. On the recording, which still exists, Browning recites part of How They Brought the Good News from Ghent to Aix, and can even be heard apologising when he forgets the words.

The recording was first played in 1890 on the anniversary of his death, at a gathering of his admirers, it was said to be the first time anyone's voice 'had been heard from beyond the grave'.

His last work Asolando: Fancies and Facts (1889), returned to his brief and concise lyric verse that was so popular. It was published on the day of his death on December 12th, 1889, Robert Browning was at his son's home Ca' Rezzonico in Venice.

He was buried in Poets' Corner in Westminster Abbey; his grave lies immediately adjacent to that of Alfred Tennyson.

Among the many who have publicly acknowledged their literary debt to him are Henry James, Oscar Wilde, George Bernard Shaw, G. K. Chesterton, Ezra Pound, Jorge Luis Borges, and Vladimir Nabokov.

Robert Browning - A Concise Bibliography

Here follows a list of the plays and poetry volumes published during his lifetime. Poems of particular worth are noted from within those volumes.

Pauline: A Fragment of a Confession (1833)
Paracelsus (1835)
Strafford (play) (1837)
Sordello (1840)

Bells and Pomegranates No. I: Pippa Passes (play) (1841)
  The Year's at the Spring
Bells and Pomegranates No. II: King Victor and King Charles (play) (1842)
Bells and Pomegranates No. III: Dramatic Lyrics (1842)
  Porphyria's Lover
  Soliloquy of the Spanish Cloister
  My Last Duchess
  The Pied Piper of Hamelin
  Count Gismond
  Johannes Agricola in Meditation
Bells and Pomegranates No. IV: The Return of the Druses (play) (1843)
Bells and Pomegranates No. V: A Blot in the 'Scutcheon (play) (1843)
Bells and Pomegranates No. VI: Colombe's Birthday (play) (1844)
Bells and Pomegranates No. VII: Dramatic Romances and Lyrics (1845)
  The Laboratory
  How They Brought the Good News from Ghent to Aix
  The Bishop Orders His Tomb at Saint Praxed's Church
  The Lost Leader
  Home Thoughts from Abroad
  Meeting at Night
Bells and Pomegranates No. VIII: Luria and A Soul's Tragedy (plays) (1846)
Christmas-Eve and Easter-Day (1850)
An Essay on Percy Bysshe Shelley (essay) (1852)
Two Poems (1854)
Men and Women (1855)
  Love Among the Ruins
  A Toccata of Galuppi's
  Childe Roland to the Dark Tower Came
  Fra Lippo Lippi
  Andrea Del Sarto
  The Patriot
  The Last Ride Together
  Memorabilia
  Cleon
  How It Strikes a Contemporary
  The Statue and the Bust
  A Grammarian's Funeral
  An Epistle Containing the Strange Medical Experience of Karshish, the Arab Physician
  Bishop Blougram's Apology
  Master Hugues of Saxe-Gotha
  By the Fire-side
Dramatis Personae (1864)
  Caliban upon Setebos
  Rabbi Ben Ezra
  Abt Vogler
  Mr. Sludge, "The Medium"
  Prospice
  A Death in the Desert

The Ring and the Book (1868–69)
Balaustion's Adventure (1871)
Prince Hohenstiel-Schwangau, Saviour of Society (1871)
Fifine at the Fair (1872)
Red Cotton Night-Cap Country, or, Turf and Towers (1873)
Aristophanes' Apology (1875)
 Thamuris Marching
The Inn Album (1875)
Pacchiarotto, and How He Worked in Distemper (1876)
 Numpholeptos
The Agamemnon of Aeschylus (1877)
La Saisiaz and The Two Poets of Croisic (1878)
Dramatic Idylls (1879)
Dramatic Idylls: Second Series (1880)
 Pan and Luna
Jocoseria (1883)
Ferishtah's Fancies (1884)
Parleyings with Certain People of Importance in Their Day (1887)
Asolando (1889)
 Prologue
 Summum Bonum
 Bad Dreams III
 Flute-Music, with an Accompaniment
 Epilogue

www.ingramcontent.com/pod-product-compliance
Lightning Source LLC
Chambersburg PA
CBHW060130050426

42448CB00010B/2060

* 9 7 8 1 7 8 7 3 7 6 3 9 7 *